Exploring
Felting

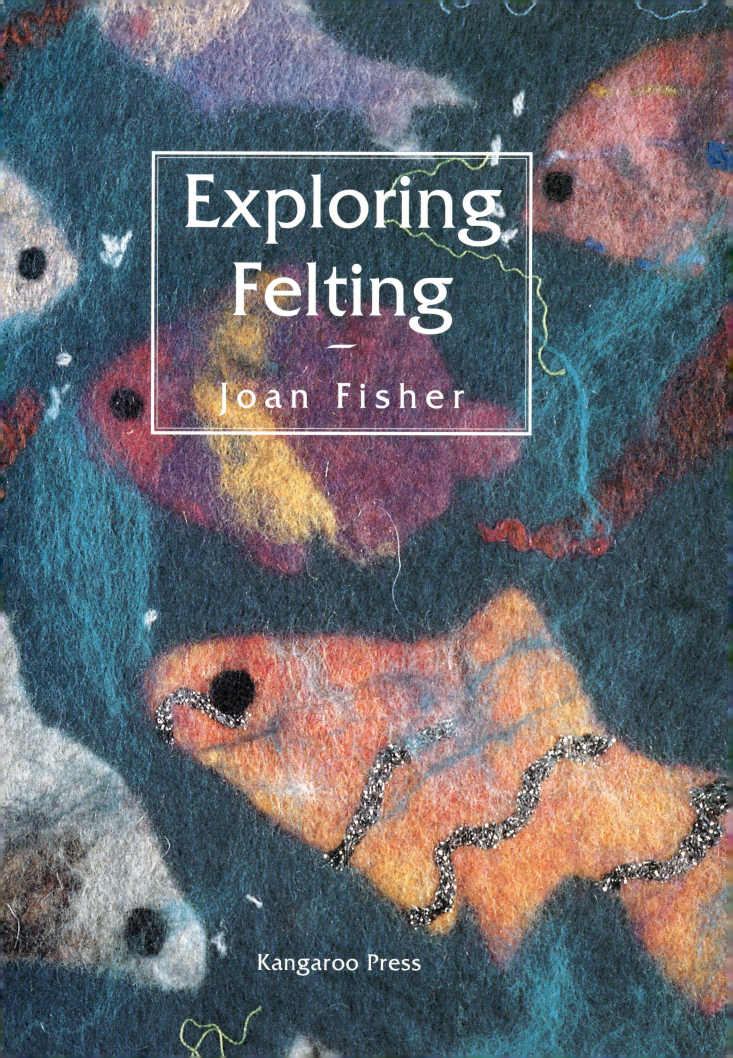

Exploring Felting

Joan Fisher

Kangaroo Press

Dedication

To my grandchildren Alice, Ruth, Ella and Ky Andrew
and the next generation
who will continue the good work of creating beautiful
things with this ancient craft.

Acknowledgments

My thanks:

To Jean Dawson for the many hours spent on the
computer preparing my notes for the editor.

To Eardley Lancaster for the photography.

To Jenny Hopper for her clear description of 'How and
Why Wool Fibres Felt'.

To Brigitte Perik for the trouble she took to find the
relevant areas in the school syllabus where the
teaching of felting would be an advantage.

To Liz Calnan, Joyce Darley, Carol Divall and Christine
Sloan who generously allowed me to use photographs
of their work to show you the endless possibilities of
felting.

To Alan Tremain who first suggested this book and
encouraged me to attempt it.

Without the encouragement of friends this book could
never have been written.

Cover photograph: Pisces coat by Joan Fisher.
Photo courtesy June Underwood, South Tamworth.

Title page: Detail of Pisces coat.

First published in 1997 by Kangaroo Press Pty Ltd
An imprint of Simon & Schuster Australia
20 Barcoo Street (PO Box 507)
East Roseville NSW 2069 Australia
Printed in Hong Kong through Colorcraft Ltd

ISBN 0 86417 857 3

Contents

Hand painted vest with resist pockets by Joan Fisher

Foreword

A craft book?

Yes, a recipe book for the creative mind!

Anybody interested in felting may start without previous training in this craft, one of the oldest known to humanity.

Joan, you are demonstrating your achievements step by step in every detail. You have become the teacher and now I will be one of your pupils.

The love for wool brought me to Australia; it is the medium for most of us most readily available for felting, although there are other materials as well that will felt. You are guiding the novice carefully through the process and do not leave the development to chance. The child and the adult, the dilettante and the craftsman / artist, all will benefit from your book according to their creativity and need.

In this day and age, where the forming of groups has become so important, I visualise that this felting activity, apart from producing practical and beautiful articles, will also act as a healing art therapy. This is living! Learn something new at different stages throughout your life.

Thank you, Joan, for including me in your project and for your enthusiasm. I will keep on experimenting myself, I promise. Best wishes for your next initiative.

Erica Semler

Past artist-in-residence at the University of New England, Armidale
Sponsored by the Australian Council of Arts
Master Weaver, foundation and life member of the
Handweavers & Spinners Guild of NSW

'Rainforest': wall-hanging by Joan Fisher; detail on right shows the depth of perspective

Introduction

This book is written for all those people who love working with natural fibres and making them into beautiful and useful articles. I trust it will be an exciting introduction to felting techniques, inspiring you to a lifetime of creative enjoyment. Once you feel confident with the techniques I describe, open your mind to the possibilities and put part of yourself into your creations. We have been told that God created us in his own image—so, of course, we all have the ability to create. Just find your medium and give it everything you have got.

Many are the stories of the origin of felting, but we know it goes back to prehistoric times. Possibly, as one legend suggests, people cushioned their feet with animal wool or hair and through the action of body heat and moisture felt was created. Certainly felt is the oldest fabric and has been used for millenia for many items including tents, clothing and blankets.

For over twenty years I have been a spinner and weaver, and thirteen years ago Erica Semler introduced me to the joys of felting when I attended one of her workshops. Spinning and weaving require a great deal of patience, and articles made this way take time. A felted article, on the other hand, can be completed in one day, indeed, even in one hour. Spinning and weaving require expensive equipment, while felting can be done on the kitchen table using simply water, soap, fleece and lots of enthusiasm.

Even if you find your initial efforts tiring, practice will improve your style and all the felt you make will find remarkable uses. The feet of my kitchen table were making marks on the linoleum floor, so I made them little felt slippers, and the problem was solved. Likewise felt glued to the feet of my weaving seat in another room protected the parquetry floor from scratches.

Cushions and rugs, clothing, hats and slippers can all be made from felt. Felt can be made thick and heavy and rugged enough for floorcovering, or almost tissue-thin for the lightest of scarves or a lampshade. It's amazing what can be made from felt—I remember in one of my workshops a student arrived with a pattern for an engine gasket: her husband was delighted when she made him exactly what he required.

Children love making felt; they can do it in the backyard without worrying about mess, and it will occupy them for hours. Group felting can draw friends to design and make large rugs, or wall-hangings, which are often sought for local public buildings. A magnificent wall-hanging in Newcastle called 'The Valley' uses felt in a collage.

I hope this book will be of special interest to country folk who run their own animals and need another outlet for their product. Craft centres and gift shops are always looking for locally made articles

Children laying down fleece . . . and rolling up the matchstick blind

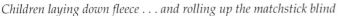

9

with a difference. The chapter on Small Items and Gifts gives you ways to make use of offcuts from large items and all those samples that end up stacked away to 'do something with'—so there need be no waste!

I use mostly wool and animal fibres in my felting. I have tried flax alone as well but the finished product is more like handmade paper, lacking the flexibility of felts made from animal sources. Wool and wool blends are by far the easiest fibres to work with, but experimenting is great fun. Silk, mohair, cashmere, angora and flax all blend beautifully with wool and give an exquisite finish, while cashmere and mohair felt well on their own.

Whatever you are thinking of using, make a sample first, before you decide whether the felt suits the project that you have in mind. Making a sample may seem tedious but experience has shown me that it saves time in the end.

If you happen to be working with children in a school or in a holiday centre, it may take more than one period or session to finish a project. The project can be laid down in the first session, rolled up in a blind and secured well with rubbber bands. Next session, wet it down through the blind and complete the felting process.

I have ordered the projects by their degree of difficulty. If you begin with flat felting and work your way through the book, you will be delighted with the results you achieve.

May this book soon become dog-eared and well used as you explore this ancient craft. Enjoy yourself and I will consider the effort taken in writing this book worthwhile.

Children of all ages can felt. Start with small items such as balls and allow the children to select yarns and colours to create their own balls. Tiny balls threaded onto strong twine make a necklace that will delight little girls. Boys revel in making masks, attached over the ears with elastic bands.

Embroidery enhances felt. Small strips of felt embroidered and made into serviette rings are fun to work and make attractive gifts.

Wall-hangings can be enhanced with added embroidery, beads, sequins, shells, buttons and other adornments to give interest and depth to their designs. Other variations include laying down layers of different coloured fleece. When felted and dried, cut down with a sharp blade to reveal the under layers. The use of resists can create pockets and unusual effects.

For clothing I aim for a fine, soft drapeable fabric, very evenly felted. If you are making a garment in felt, a simple design will show off beautiful felt best. Choose a design to suit the fabric.

Good finishing really sets off a piece of felting. Take the trouble to line jackets properly, tack edges carefully and steam press. Be fussy with buttonholes and buttons. Make them a feature. Buttons made of natural materials such as wood, bone or pearlshell look best with handmade felt.

The nature of felt means that stitches can be hidden in the thickness. Felt can also be stretched into curves and mounds that no other fabric can achieve.

To keep up with the latest techniques it is well worthwhile meeting with other felters. See if you can find a group to join. I have always found the exchange of ideas is invaluable.

For bibliography and a list for further reading turn to page 90. You will also find a list of tutors and a list of suppliers and carders at the back of the book.

- O N E -

Getting started

Fleeces

Understanding why wool felts is esssential for good results. The success of felting lies in the quality of the fleece that is used. A fleece is the whole coat of a sheep, made up of many staples. A staple is a small section of the fleece containing many fibres, which become entangled during the felting process. Each fibre has small scales or serrations, overlapping and facing to the tip of the staple.

The entangling of the serrations is only part of the felting process, however. More important is the core of the fibre, which has an elastic quality that reacts when the surface tension of the fibre is broken by the application of soap and hot water; the fibre reacts by folding back on itself. If you lay down two layers of different colours, when you felt them you will see how the fibres travel and entwine. As the elasticity of human skin decreases with age, so it is with wool. Fleeces from old sheep should not be used for felting,

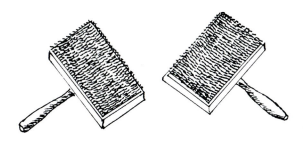

Hand carders

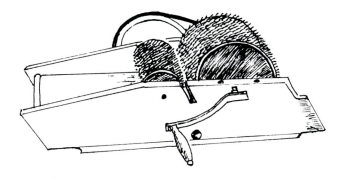

A drum carder

Matchstick blind, sheeting and wooden felting tool

as you will probably finish up with a spongy pressed wool instead of a firm felted wool. For a more thorough explanation see Appendix 1 on page 84.

Take time to prepare your wool, washing and cleaning it thoroughly. See page 15 for instructions on washing a dirty fleece. Thoroughly skirt the fleece (removing soiled staples around the edges), then remove dust and foreign matter by giving the fleece a gentle shake. Good preparation will save time.

If I am carding my own fleece I prefer to use a hand carder, which is excellent for fine felt and blending in other fibres. Drum carders are much quicker, but it is harder to produce batts of approximately the same size. Prepare the complete quantity you think you will need before you start felting.

For your first attempts at felting I would suggest you use commercially prepared wool, which is easier to lay down than hand carded wool, and will give you confidence. There are many reliable suppliers (see page 93) and you have the choice of fleeces from many breeds.

Merino with its fine crimp and softness is perhaps the most successful felting breed, but fleeces from many breeds felt well, even some of the long-haired, coarse varieties.

Always make a sample before starting a project. Consider what kind of wool is best suited to the article you are planning—fine wools for garments and strong wools for slippers, bags and other articles that may have to cope with a lot of friction.

Working surface

A comfortable working area is essential. Laying large items out on the ground is possible, but can be back-breaking.

A large kitchen table, or a table-tennis table covered with a waterproof material and steadied with extra support, make excellent large work areas. The addition of masonite sheets can extend the size for preliminary laying down. The rug on pages 67–69 was made using this method. As the felting progresses the size of the piece reduces and thus it becomes more manageable. If a very large piece of felt is planned, remember that it is possible to felt in two layers separated by cloth. This will help turn out larger pieces on your kitchen table.

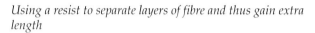

Using a resist to separate layers of fibre and thus gain extra length

Felting agents

Soaps and detergents are both used as agents in the felting process; you will soon find out which you prefer. I favour a good, pure, laundry soap or soap flakes. You need something which is gentle on your hands, unless you like wearing rubber gloves. I chop the soap and place it into a large jar—2 cakes to 2 litres (8 cups) of hot water. I use half a cup of the resulting jelly to 1 litre (4 cups) of hot water for wetting down the prepared fleece. You will learn from experience when the amounts are right.

Other equipment

Pieces of old sheeting or light curtain fabrics are necessary for the initial stages of felting to cover the fleece before you wet it down. A felting tool, a smooth rectangular block of wood with a handle, is invaluable for distributing the soap solution evenly on large pieces.

I prefer a matchstick blind for rolling the felt; for me it is the quickest and easiest method. I have blinds in several sizes, including a small one for sampling. The one I usually work with measures 155 cm x 92 cm (60" x 36" approximately). This gives me a roll at each end, as I work in the middle section.

Shaping the felt

I rarely use needle and thread to stitch my fleece in the covering material, for I constantly look at my progress, turning in the edges and following the pattern. Simple items made by children could be stitched to keep the pad in place, and allow for the energetic treatment children love to give.

If you prefer not to work with a blind, try covering your pad with a length of the porous woven plastic called Weed Mat, available at plant nurseries. Then work in the soap solution with the felting tool, massaging vigorously. A felting rolling pin is also helpful. It may take a little longer but the result should be the same.

Laying down

Learning to lay down an even batt with no thin areas is the secret of good felting. The trick is to not handle too much fibre at one time, keeping the piece over the top of your hand so it does not drag over the pad. Flick your hand up after each piece is pulled, so that the fibres separate and fall on the pad openly and evenly. Practice will make perfect!

All weights given are for clean carded fleece. You will need more if you are starting with unwashed fleece. Merino wool weighs less than stronger fleeces, so to be on the safe side allow a little extra if you are working with it.

Sampling

The first step with any felting project is to make the sample. Open your blind leaving a roll at each end. A 25 cm (10") sample is a sufficient size and is large enough to be made into a useful item later.

If you are using staples of fleece (uncarded fleece), flick or comb them, then draw off a fine layer with your thumb and the side of your hand as shown in the diagram.

Throughout this book I will refer to top to bottom as north to south (N/S) and to side to side as east to west (E/W) as the directions for laying your fleece.

Start laying the fleece from north to south (N/S), overlapping both tops and sides, and using a 25 cm (10") square pattern to obtain an accurate shape.

The second layer of the fleece is laid in the same way, but this time from east to west (E/W). It is important to keep the pad even.

If you are using carded fleece, the principle is the same. Tearing off a narrow strip first helps; then draw

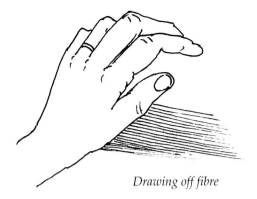

Drawing off fibre

Laying down wool at right angles; the layers are placed on top of each other

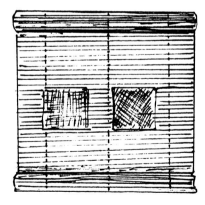

Matchstick blind set up with samples

needs more felting

felted

Pinch or tent test

off a small amount from it and place it in the same manner. The occasional grass seed can be removed when the felt is dry, with a pair of tweezers, much the same as removing a splinter from a finger.

The carded wool tops that come in long slivers or rolags make laying down easy.

Laying down two samples straight onto the blind, with different numbers of layers, will give you a comparison and help you decide on the suitability for your project. If you intend adding other fibres or colours do so on your samples.

Sampling will also tell you how much felting is needed. Sometimes a sheer, soft felt can be made with little effort, where to overfelt would make it hard. Once again the final use must be kept in mind. Even if you are unhappy with the way the sample comes out, remember there is no such thing as unusable felt. There is always some exciting way to use what you have made.

Once you have the sample pad laid down, with the density as even as you can get, cover it with a soft cloth, folding under at the edges, and damp the pad down with hot soap and water mixture, using a ½ cup of soap jelly to 1 litre (4 cups) of hot water. Pour the mixture gently into the middle of the pad and softly pat outwards to the edges, then distribute the moisture evenly with a felting tool. If you have laid down an intricate pattern, cover it with a plastic mesh and rub over the surface with the felting tool to set the pattern before rolling. Merino tends to wrinkle if it is not partly felted before rolling, so it's generally better to follow this procedure with Merino even if there is no pattern.

Roll the blind by lifting and rolling, lifting and rolling, so that you do not distort the pad. Roll gently and unroll and inspect frequently for wrinkles.

As soon as the water has removed all the air from the fibres, and the pad is evenly damp and smooth to the touch, even up the edges by turning them under to the size of the sample or the pattern. Continue to roll with a rhythmic action, using the weight of your shoulders. With practice and using the correct method your arms should not tire. There is no guide for length of time in felting. This depends entirely on the fleece and the manner of felting.

It is important to inspect the pad frequently. When the fleece is matting together remove the cover cloth and turn the sample 90°. Shrinkage occurs in the direction of rolling, so frequent turning of the sample will give even felt.

The felt is ready for fulling when the fibres are firm. Test by pinching up a little tent as in the diagram. If the fibres are still loose and come up too easily, more rolling and perhaps more soap is needed. You should have adequate soap lather but not an excess of water. The picture on page 34 will give you an idea of 'adequate' lather.

Keep a sponge or cloth nearby to mop up extra water. The table should be wet but not so wet that water is running off onto the floor. Too much water floats the fibres and prevents the felting process taking place.

There is a moment in all felting when you wonder what this mess is, but it is only a moment and it passes quickly as the joy of felting overwhelms you.

Fulling

Fulling is rinsing the felt once in hot then cold water. A dash of vinegar in the final rinse clears away any residual soap.

Slamming it down on a draining board, as part of the process, helps to harden and fix the felt. This is a great time to get rid of your frustrations. If you have been tense and under pressure **slam** that wool down. (With exclamations if necessary, ensuring that the family is out of earshot!)

Fulling can also be done in the rinse cycle of the washing machine but be careful doing it this way— you can go beyond the point you want to achieve and finish with too-hard felt. Check frequently for the degree of felting you require.

Drying

The piece of felt can now be placed on a towel, put back in the blind and gently rolled to remove unevennesses, and surplus water. This gives you a smooth fabric ready for drying.

If you intend to dry the felt in a clothes-dryer be prepared for further shrinkage. You may need to iron the felt after this.

Draping it over the clothes-line to dry will keep the shape and softness and eliminate the need to iron, or you can lay it flat over chicken netting or even a clean trampoline.

For clothing I try to achieve a soft, fine, drapeable fabric, evenly felted with no thin areas. If, on lifting the fabric to the light you have weak areas, turn to Chapter 11 on troubleshooting for advice.

Preparation of fleece

Selecting a fleece for felting

Fleece can be tested for its felting capacity before you buy. (The conscientious felter will keep a small bottle of soap and water solution in one pocket when looking for good fleece to buy.) Take a small amount of the wool and roll it in the palm of your hand with a few drops of soap solution. A satisfactory test will quickly result in the fleece turning into a small, hard ball.

If you cannot buy and test the fleece in person, buying through a trustworthy, tried supplier is the alternative. (See suppliers list on page 93.)

Washing a greasy fleece

A raw fleece should be skirted before you buy it. Skirting is the removal of all matted, stained, grass or seed-filled wool from the fleece.

A good supplier will always sell you a clean fleece. Some suppliers, growing wool especially for craft people, even rug their sheep to protect the fleece from dirt. Though this fleece is more expensive, it is a joy to use.

To wash a greasy fleece, fill a plastic bucket with hand-hot water and use a tablespoon of my favourite wool-wash recipe, or a good commercial substitute.

Wool-wash
500 g (16 oz) soap flakes
25 ml (5 teaspoons) eucalyptus oil
125 ml (½ cup) methylated spirits
Mix well and store in screw-top jars.

Mix the wool-wash thoroughly in the hand-hot water, then add enough of the fleece to fill the bucket, ensuring that it is completely submerged. (You will need anything between 4 and 8 buckets if you want to do a whole fleece at the one time. This allows the sorting of fleece from different parts of the body; the neck and shoulders give the best quality fleece, then the sides and back, then the legs and stomach, especially the finer, shorter fibres.) Leave the fleece to soak for at least half an hour, or overnight.

Upturn the bucket into the sink and press out the water using the bottom of the bucket. It is wise not to agitate the fleece during the washing process, as this will tangle the fibres.

Rinsing

Fill the bucket with warm water, submerge the fleece for a few minutes, drain and press out the water as before. A dirty, dusty fleece may need a second rinse.

Drying

If you can find an old refrigerator shelf or a piece of strong wire mesh, allow the fleece to drip dry on this. I place my 'drying shelf' on the rotary clothes hoist, turning the fleece over as it dries. As the fleece dries it will increase in volume.

Spin-drying (not tumble-drying) the rinsed fleece in a mesh bag before laying it out to dry will hasten the procedure. Turn off the rinse-spray cycle since this can cause felting.

Storage

Store the clean dried fleece in a cardboard box. Pull each staple separately from the fleece and lay them in the box, with a few mothballs for protection.

Other fibres suitable for felting

Mohair, alpaca, camel, angora, flax and certain breeds of dog-hair blended with wool make beautiful felt. Some of these fibres felt quite well alone, but here again sampling is a necessity. (Many of these fibres can be purchased through the suppliers listed on pages 93–95.)

Surface additions

Silk carded in with Merino wool gives a sheen missing in Merino wool. Laying just a little silk in the final layer will enhance most felts.

If you have silk cocoons, tease them out and felt the whole cocoon as a design feature.

Baby mohair felts well as a surface feature. The soft curls make wonderful fringes and highlights.

The man's blue vest on page 31 was worked with two layers of wool with a third layer of mohair, then decorated with an exotic mohair and silk commercial yarn.

Yarns, embroidery threads, machine threads, lurex threads, tapestry wool and all knitting yarns when used discreetly will add dimension and charm to felt.

Surface designs can be random and abstract, or very specific, even pictorial. You can draw a complex design on a soft base cloth and lay down decorative fibres following the design, adjusting them until you are satisfied with the shapes and the depth of colour. Then add layers N/S and E/W to the thickness you desire. Laying the design down first will give you a mirror image, as in the wall-hanging in Chapter 9 (page 60).

To hold additions to the surface draw out a gossamer amount of fleece and lay it over the design to anchor the threads to the surface.

Carding

Carding opens up and aerates the fibres and lays them parallel to each other. There are three methods of carding.

1. Flicking with a wire flicker or dog's comb, good for small quantities.
2. Handcarders (as used by spinners) are excellent for blending fibres. The resulting rolags can be stored in a cardboard box in the same way as staples.
3. Drum carding: Using a drum carder you can do large quantities of fleece in less time.

If the fleece has been stored for a long period and feels hard, place it in the sun or warm it beside a heater or oven, to soften the oil and make handling easier.

For beginners and people intending to go into production, the quickest way of getting started is to have your fleece carded professionally or to buy carded wool from a reputable supplier. (See suppliers, pages 93–95.)

Density

To work the projects in this book successfully you will need a guide to density—three layers for a sheer scarf will differ from three layers for a floor mat.

To help uniformity, draw off the fleece with the side of your hand, holding it between the thumb and forefinger. If you are using tops (prepared wool), you can divide each tops into two or three.

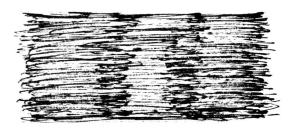

Indication of density—fine, medium and thick layers

Density guide

Fine layer: A gossamer amount that, placed on this page, will still permit the print to be read.

Medium layer: This amount will obscure the print but allow you to see the spaces.

Thick layer: This amount will completely obscure the page—type and all.

Your aim is to lay down an even pad of fibre, with no thin areas and with even edges. This way you will have no waste.

With experience, you will be able to judge the finished thickness of the felt quite accurately from the pad. Feel the pad between your thumb and finger, pressing them together firmly to gauge the final thickness. Estimating from the height of the pad alone can be misleading, as some fleece packs down more than others.

Setting a pattern

Covering the layered fleece with a damp cloth and lightly pressing, using a hot iron, with an up and down motion, lays the fibres and anchors them. This can be especially important when including a regular pattern in the felt.

GUARDING AGAINST INJURY

Your back can be under strain if you do not listen to its complaints, especially when laying down large pieces. Too low a table can tempt you into reaching too far over it. Any table that you can span will give your back some twitches if you do not take precautions.

My kitchen table is 80 cm x 122 cm (32" x 48" approximately) and has bench type seats each side. I rest my knees on the bench as I move along laying down my fleece. As I reach over, the weight of my body comes onto my knees, not my spine. Without this advantage, try bending your knees with feet well apart to take the weight.

Be aware of the potential for back strain and I am sure you will devise a relief plan.

Stop every now and then, relax and flex the muscles, shake the hands and deep breathe.

OTHER PRECAUTIONS

Never work with unwashed fleece on your kitchen table; any soiled material should be prepared and felted outside. Remember the kitchen table is for serving family meals. As a precaution, always clean up and wipe work surfaces with a mild disinfectant.

Keeping your tetanus vaccinations up to date is essential if you are handling raw fleeces. (Spinners always take this precaution.)

If you use an electric sander to hasten the felting process, remember that caution should always be taken when using electricity near water. A circuit-breaker or a safety switch is a sensible precaution. I rarely find occasion to use the sander, keeping it mainly for very large pieces and for welding seams together.

To protect the sander from water, I have made a heavy duty plastic cover for it. The cover must not exclude the flow of air or you risk burning out the motor. Even a shower cap under the sander will keep the tool dry.

Quantities given in the projects are the minimum, so as a beginner allow extra until you have mastered the technique. Remember good felting quality wool makes the best felt.

THREE

Flat felting

Project 1: Shoulder bag

YOU WILL NEED:
200–250 g (6–8 oz) carded wool
extra pieces of coloured wool or fleece or other
    fibres
piece of sheeting or fine cloth approximately 110 cm x
    70 cm (43" x 27")
soap solution
matchstick blind

First, make a 25 cm (10") sample using 4 layers of
medium density. See page 16. Add random colour
and texture to the surface of the sample. When the
sample is finished, following the main instructions
below, record the amount of shrinkage, the number
of layers and the fibres used.

Shoulder bag

METHOD
With the knowledge gained from the sample in mind,
lay down three or four medium layers approximately
100 cm x 60 cm (40" x 24"). Lay down a design of
your choice on top of the final layer with the extra
coloured wool or fibre. Uncarded staples will give
an attractive curly effect. If you use other fibres with
low felting quality as part of the surface design, you
can make sure they felt into the work by laying
superfine layers of wool over the design at random.

If you want to make a strong carrying bag but don't
want to line it, try placing a piece of tulle between
the second and third layers. Soft bridal tulle (cotton
or silk) felts best. Synthetics will not bond with
natural fibres.

Lay the pad directly onto the matchstick blind,
cover with a cloth and wet down, patting the
moisture out to the edges.

After the initial rolling to even out the moisture,
turn in the edges to neaten them.

If you laid down a coloured design in the first layer,
turn the edges of the felt over to the top. If your design
was in the last layer you laid down, the edges should
be turned under.

With wet fingers, pat and straighten the edges, and
fold the fibre over or under as needed to give the
edges a neat finish.

Continue to roll, turning the piece 90° when it is
holding together. Keep felting until it passes the tent
test (page 13) and is firm enough for your needs. This
could take anything from 15 to 45 minutes.

Full as described on page 14, rinse, roll in a towel
or spin dry.

MAKING UP THE BAG
If you wish, press the felt on the wrong side using an
iron over a damp cloth.

Cut a shoulder strap from the long edge of the
rectangle, or two handles for a tote bag.

If you decide to line the bag, a zippered pocket in
the lining is a useful extra.

Machine the seams, using a double row of stitching
to hold the handles.

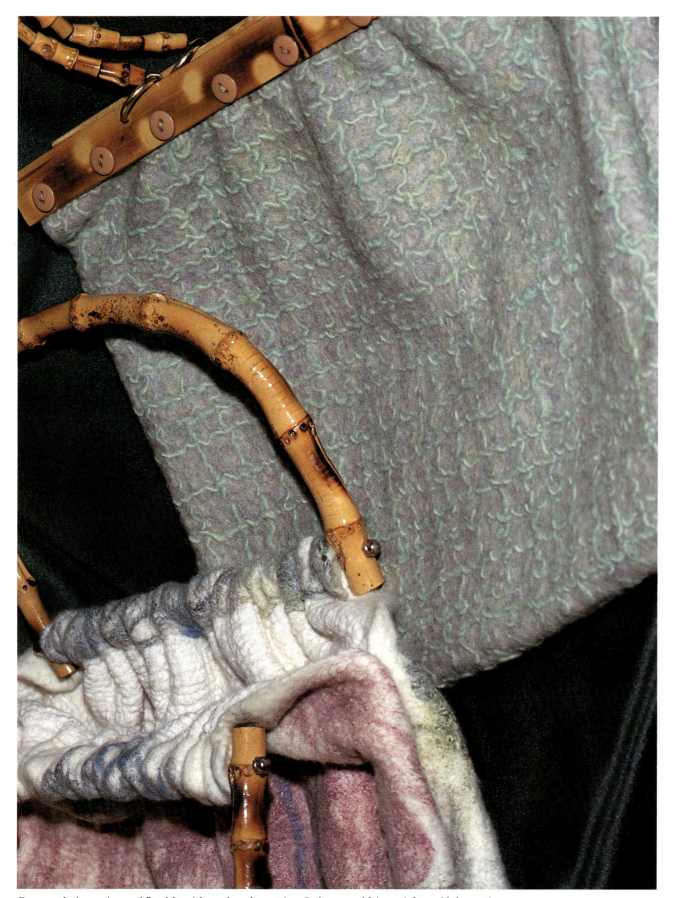

Bags made from pieces of flat felt with surface decoration. Left: nuno felting; right: grid decoration

Project 2: Scarf

YOU WILL NEED:
60–100 g (2–3 oz) fine Merino wool, washed and carded
two pieces of fine, soft cloth, 120 cm x 18 cm (48" x 7"), the other 144 cm x 32 cm (57" x 12½")
soap solution
matchstick blind

The success of a scarf lies in its softness. Before settling on the fibre, take a handful and gently rub it under your chin. If it feels prickly, reject it for scarf making.

Make a sample following the main instructions, laying down three 'fine' layers. Add wisps of silk and/or mohair. Analyse the finished sample, recording shrinkage and strength and noting any thin areas.

Laying down two narrow scarves for felting simultaneously

METHOD
Lay the larger piece of cloth on the blind. With knowledge of the sample in mind, lay down three 'fine' layers, being careful not to create thin areas. Add a pattern of contrast colours or fibres.

Keep the pad within the area of the cloth pattern, and make it a little finer towards the edges.

Cover with the second cloth and wet down with the soap and water solution. Gently roll to evenly distribute the moisture. Unroll and turn under the edges to neaten. Fold the cloth over the edges and damp down evenly.

Continue to roll gently until the felt is firm. Turn the scarf 90°, folding it over the cloth if the width of the blind is insufficient. The cloth acts as a resist to prevent the scarf felting together on itself. Continue felting and turning until the scarf is the desired length and width. Do a pinch test to make sure the fibres are firm.

Full as described on page 14, placing in hot, then cold, water. Place on a towel, ease into shape, then roll with a rolling pin or use the blind to squeeze out the water. Hang to dry.

For a longer scarf you can set up two batts (pads), separated by a cloth. Wet down the first batt of three layers, place the cloth in position, fold a small amount of the batt over the edge of the cloth, then continue laying the rest of the scarf with the cloth acting as a resist (see diagram on page 12). Wet down with the solution and felt.

You can felt double the size of your felting area with this method.

Fine Merino scarf trimmed with a knotted fringe

Merino scarf in jewel colours with fringe of mohair staples felted into the ends

Variation Mohair staples can be used for a fringe if you wish. When laying down the scarf at the beginning, place the mohair staples between the second and third layers, including one-third of the length of the staple in the end of the scarf. Felt in the cut ends; the weathered tips do not felt as well. Wrap the rest of the fringe in a cloth resist to prevent it felting together.

Project 3: Stole (sheer felting)

YOU WILL NEED:
100–120 g (3–4 oz) soft carded fleece
length of fabric the size of the stole, 160 cm x 40 cm (63" x 16")
large piece of cloth, 180 cm x 50 cm (70" x 20")
decorative elements—pieces of silk, mohair, glitter thread or any suitable contrast
soap solution
matchstick blind

Make a 25 cm (10") sample to test thickness, colour, suitable contrasts and textures. Two 'fine' layers of fleece should be sufficient, with a decorative layer top and bottom.

A felted stole so sheer that the model's hair shows through

METHOD
Spread the larger piece of cloth on the matchstick blind. Lay down the decorative materials for the design. If you have drawn a design on the cloth, wet down the materials with the solution or anchor them with a sheet of glass as you move along.

Add the first fine layer of fleece, then the second layer at right angles. Check for thin areas, and add the upper design elements. The design on the top layer can reinforce weak areas, and balance the thicknesses of the first design.

You now have a decorative layer, a first fine layer overlapping the edges, a second fine layer at right angles and a finishing decorative layer. A fringe could be felted in, or added later.

Check again for thin spots, cover with the piece of fabric the same size as the finished stole, and damp down with the soap and water solution.

Gently roll to even out the moisture, being careful that there are no dry spots.

Unroll the blind and turn in the edges of the stole. Continue to roll and turn at 90° until the fabric is firm. Insert a cloth resist if felting double.

This sheer felt is soft and drapes well, but great care must be taken in the laying down to prevent holes appearing. (You can see from the photograph how sheer it is.)

After the initial wetting down, a little fleece can be added if obvious holes appear, but once felting has begun, follow the instructions on page 77 on troubleshooting to make repairs.

Full gently and roll in a towel, easing to the finished size. Drape over the line to dry.

Ironing softly with a damp cloth may improve the finished stole. Add a fringe now if you didn't choose to felt one in, and any surface decorations of glitter threads, beads, plaits or knots to enhance its appearance.

Project 4: Dress and suit lengths

A 10–12 size dress can be made from three pieces of felt each measuring 70 cm x 100 cm (28″ x 40″). (See the pink suit.) If your size and pattern call for another piece of felt, this is where sampling, and recording shrinkage, can help you produce the required amount. Pattern pieces at least 2 sizes larger can be traced onto cloth and felted to the required size.

YOU WILL NEED:
750 g (25 oz) fine tops (wool blended with silk or
    mohair)
2 m (2¼ yds) bridal tulle in colour to blend
matching lining for skirt and/or jacket
sheeting or fine cloth larger than felt pieces
felting tool
soap solution
matchstick blind
cotton thread to match
buttons
zipper
light Vilene

Make a 25 cm (10″) sample, putting the tulle in the centre of four fine layers. The purpose of the tulle is to prevent the finished garment developing stretched patches in areas such as the elbows or seat. Use soft bridal tulle, *not* the stiff tulle. It is important to make a sample to make sure the fibre felts into the tulle. Stretch the tulle slightly to avoid wrinkles in the felting.

Check to see that the finished cloth is the thickness you require; you may have to adjust the density of the layers to suit your needs. My fabric was approximately 3 mm (1/8″) thick.

METHOD
Lay direct onto blind, taking time to make the layers even. Lay the first layer E/W, the second layer N/S. Cover with the tulle, easing the tulle to avoid wrinkles. Put down the third layer E/W, the fourth N/S.

Cover with large damp cloth. Wet down with soap solution, distributing it evenly with a felting tool.

Felt in usual way, turning 90° when felt is holding together.

Working on my kitchen table, which is 80 cm x 120 cm (32″ x 48″), with fine tops, gives me a finished piece 70 cm x 100 cm (28″ x 40″).

A fine felt of blended wool, silk and mohair made into a classic suit

The pieces must be well felted or else they will pill in the wearing of the garment. Pills or balls on felt have to be picked off, as brushing only brings up the pile.

Full and dry the felt and lightly press on the wrong side using a damp cloth. Store on a cardboard roller until you are ready to make up the garment.

Alternative: You can felt the bodice as for a vest, placing the fronts to each side of the back and folding in the neck and armholes. This does save some wool and is an exciting technique. See page 51 for more information. I leave out the tulle in this method.

The weight of the finished skirt with lining and zipper is approximately 210 g (8 oz).

The jacket weighs 230 g (9 oz), including embroidered felt collar and buttons.

THE COLLAR

Cut pattern and design position of felt motifs. Mine were four-petalled flowers and leaves. Trace pattern onto tissue paper and tack onto a piece of tulle and Solvy (water-soluble fabric). Leave space around the pattern so the fabric can be stretched over the embroidery hoop. (Kristine Dibbs' *Machine Embroidery Book* is a wonderful source of information on this technique; for collar instructions see page 122.)

You will need to use the darning foot on your sewing machine. You may have to remove the foot to get the embroidery hoop in place. Adjust tension and drop the machine feed. As always, doing a small sample will give you confidence for the collar and you will see how best to use your machine.

Outline your design, securing all pieces with machine thread. I used 1.5 mm (1/16") ribbon in the machine bobbin for further decoration, but to do this you need to turn the collar over for the ribbon to be on the right side. Any random machine-stitching will add to the design. Finish the collar with a satin stitch edge.

Cut tulle and Solvy close to stitching on edge. Tear away tissue paper and wash the collar to remove the Solvy. Lay the collar on a towel, ease into shape, and dry. Gently press on wrong side and attach to neckline with a bias strip or felt facings.

(*Hint:* The water-soluble bags used for hospital laundry are bigger and cheaper than the craft fabric.)

Materials for making the embroidered collar

Detail of collar embroidery

Project 5: Bath mat with fish design

YOU WILL NEED:
250 g (8 oz) carded wool
pieces of coloured wool
ball of textured wool
small quantity coloured silk tops (optional)
sheeting or fine cloth larger than the felt pad
thick paper
plastic wrap
soap solution
matchstick blind

Make a 25 cm (10") sample to try out fibres, colours and feltability, following the main instructions.

METHOD
Draw four fish patterns on thick paper, cut out and cover with plastic wrap.

Lay down mat size directly onto the blind using three medium layers. Remember to place the layers alternately E/W and N/S. Make the layers about 10 cm (4") larger all around than the final size required, to allow for shrinkage in the felting process.

Take one of the covered fish drawings and pat down three fine layers of contrasting coloured wool. Keeping to the pattern, turn the edges. Add the eyes and any other detail. Wet down gently with your fingers. Slip the fish from the plastic into position on

'Under the sea'—exotic fish bathmat

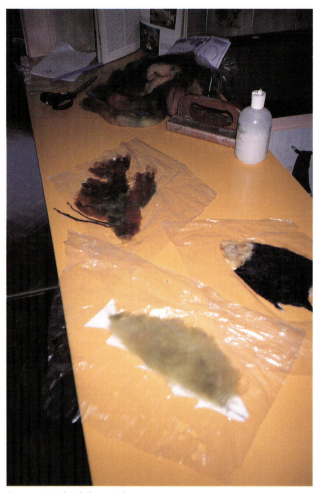

Preparing the fish motifs

the mat. Or turn the fish over and drop it onto the mat (of course, using this approach you will need to add detail and eye at this point).

Should the pad be very fluffy, you may find that placing a damp cloth on top and lightly steam pressing will give a better base for your decoration—remove the cloth and then add the design.

The fish patterns can be used over and over again, just changing their direction.

Unwind some textured wool and cut it into lengths, placing them at random on your pad to indicate water and seaweed. If you are using silk in the design, draw off very fine amounts and scatter over the bathmat.

Cover with the cloth, wet down with hot soap solution and felt in the normal way, treating the edges early in the felting process. Turn the edges under so they don't interfere with the design.

Full and dry the finished mat (see page 14).

CROCHETED EDGE
When the mat is dry thread a length of wool in an embroidery needle and do a fine line of simple chain stitch right around the edges. Each stitch needs to be long enough to take the crochet hook you are using to work the edge. Pick up each chain stitch with the hook and crochet a simple edging.

Gently press mat and edging with a damp cloth when completed.

Project 6: Inlay felting for decorative pieces

Inlay felting adds another dimension to the felting process. You can use the inlay technique on felts intended for hats, handbags, jackets, rugs and throwovers.

YOU WILL NEED:
200 g (7 oz) carded wool
selection of coloured tops

Make a 25 cm (10") sample to establish feltability of the wool and to check colour and design, following the main instructions. Is the thickness suitable for the purpose you have in mind?

METHOD
Lay down three medium layers (N/S, E/W, N/S) directly onto the matchstick blind. Cover with damp cloth and lightly press before felting.

Inlay variations Try rolling two different coloured layers of carded wool together into a sausage shape, cut it into 1 cm (3/8") thick slices and arrange in a design over the felt base. As each design is completed place a piece of heavy glass on top to set the pattern into the base. Move the glass as you proceed. Stand back and see if the design pleases you. You can add wisps of wool or silk scattered over the complete pattern, or snippets of yarn in various colours, to soften or highlight the design as well.

Cover the pad with a damp cloth and lightly press to set the pattern. Roll up the blind, lifting and rolling so as not to disturb the design.

Place rubber bands at the centre and at each end of the rolled blind. Saturate the blind with the soap solution and gently roll. You can also stand the blind in a bucket and gently pour the solution in at one end.

This colourful floral piece shows inlay work

(If hot water is not at hand, you can always use cold water—it will felt, but generally takes a little longer.)

Unroll, check the edges and neaten if necessary. If the piece is holding together turn it 90° and roll again. Place cloth resist in between folded felt if it is too wide for your blind.

Continue to roll and turn 90° until the felting test shows you have a firm felt.

Wash the felt first in hot water, then in cold. Put it back in the blind and cover with a dry towel. Roll in the blind to remove excess water and set the shape. Dry in the shade.

1. GRID INLAY PATTERN

YOU WILL NEED:
200 g (7 oz) blue-green tops
small quantity matching wool yarn
fine sheeting
soap solution
matchstick blind

Make your 25 cm (10″) sample first following the main instructions, and analyse its qualities.

METHOD
A suitable size for the pad is 100 cm x 56 cm (40″ x 22″). Lay down three medium layers of the blue-green tops on the blind—N/S, E/W, N/S.

Cut a number of yarns to equal length, and lay them down in a grid fashion—one lengthwise, one crosswise—until the whole pad is covered.

Cover pad with a damp cloth, wet down, and distribute soap solution evenly. Roll up in the blind, felt and full in the usual way.

My piece, made from crossbred tops, reduced to 60 cm x 40 cm (24″ x 16″). I used it to fashion this handbag but it would have been equally suitable for a hat.

Handbag made from felt with grid inlay pattern

2. RADIATING INLAY PATTERN

YOU WILL NEED:
100 g (3½ oz) white crossbred carded fleece
small ball navy mohair yarn
fine sheeting
soap solution
matchstick blind

Make a sample piece first, following the main instructions.

METHOD
Lay down a 76 cm (30") square of two medium layers. Following the pattern, lay in the navy yarn—first from corner to corner, then across the middle, then add a folded yarn in each eighth. With a needle and thread catch the eight loops in the middle over the crossed threads, as shown in the diagram. This thread is removed after felting. Use a few superfine wisps of fleece to anchor threads.

Cover with cloth, wet down with soap solution, and distribute the moisture evenly. Roll up in the blind and felt in the usual way. The finished size after fulling was a square of 60 cm (24").

I used this piece to make a most unusual hat (page 41), but it would also make a very interesting bag.

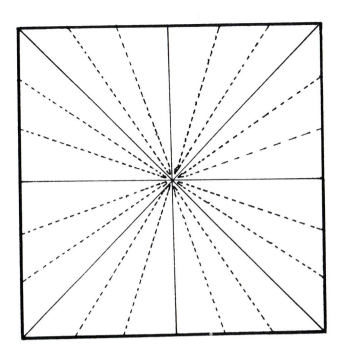

Laying down the radiating inlay

3. LEAF INLAY

YOU WILL NEED:
150 g (5 oz) brown superfine Merino tops
small quantity of white Merino staples
fine sheeting
soap solution
matchstick blind

Make a 25 cm (10") sample following the main instructions.

METHOD
Lay down two medium layers to make a pad 115 cm x 76 cm (45" x 30").

Take a piece of white staple 2 mm (1/16") thick, stretch it between your fingers, divide it into three strands, twisting the ends together to form a leaf (see detail photograph on next page).

Lay the leaf on top of the second layer; keep on adding leaves to make a border pattern on one short end of the pad.

Cover the piece with a wet cloth. A wetted cloth, having more weight, is easier to swing out and over the piece without disturbing the pattern. When covering a delicate pattern like this another pair of hands is always helpful. Pressing through the cloth with a hot iron will help to bed the pattern.

Superfine Merino has a tendency to 'ridge' during the felting process, so be careful when rolling up the blind. Check after five minutes and stretch out any creases. Fold in the edges now.

Superfine brown Merino tops made into an elegant jacket trimmed with a simple leaf pattern

Detail of leaves

When firm turn the piece 90° and felt until the tent test shows the piece is ready for fulling and drying.

Finished size is 95 cm x 63 cm (37″ x 25″). Two or three pieces will be enough to make a soft felt jacket, depending on the length of the jacket. The long jacket in the photograph took 450 g (15 oz) superfine Merino. Choose a lining fabric close to the colour of the felt.

Project 7: Blue wool and mohair man's vest

Man's vest with matching peaked cap

YOU WILL NEED:
200 g (7 oz) carded blue crossbred wool
30 g (1 oz) carded blue mohair
small ball of blue fancy mohair yarn
fine sheeting
soap solution
matchstick blind

Make a 25 cm (10") sample following the main instructions.

METHOD

Lay down two medium layers of carded wool to make a pad of 120 cm x 180 cm (48" x 71"), then one medium layer of mohair.

Cut 30 pieces of fancy mohair yarn, each 80 cm (32") long.

Lay the yarn evenly across the width of the pad in the manner shown in the photograph.

Cover with a damp cloth, and wet down with about 1.5 litres (6 cups) of hot soap solution. Gently pat down to distribute moisture evenly.

Roll in the blind for about five minutes. Unroll, straighten yarns and fold under the edges. Ease out any creases, and rewet any dry areas.

Roll again for approximately 10 minutes. Unroll and turn the piece 90°, folding over the material if it is too wide for the blind and remembering to add cloth as a resist. Roll and felt for a further 10 minutes. Try the pinch test. If further felting is required turn 90° again.

When the piece is felted to your satisfaction, full in hot then cold water. Wring, and thump on a board or the sink. Roll in a towel to remove excess water, then roll with a rolling pin to smooth and compress the fibres. I find my marble pastry rolling pin does an excellent job.

Dry the felt on the clothes line, putting a row of pegs along one side, and being careful not to crease the piece.

This felt can also be finished off in a clothes dryer, which will reduce the size further and remove loose hairs. Do not spin for too long—I recommend no more than 5 minutes.

MAKING UP

I used McCall's vest pattern No. 7365, size 120cm (48") chest to cut the vest.

Use open seams steamed flat or, if the garment is reversible, a welded seam (overlap edges and sew along each edge).

Choose appropriate buttons, natural wood or bone or felt. Felt buttons are easily made by making a long felted roll the same circumference as the buttons you want, then slicing off the number of buttons you need. Rub gently to smooth the cut edges, then either make a shank or take the thread through the button.

The darts can be pressed flat if you slit the fold. (This is not necessary if you are working with very fine felt.)

A woman's vest to fit an 82 cm (32") chest measurement, and 86 cm (34") long, can be made from a square metre (yard) of felt. New Look Pattern No. 6958 makes an attractive garment.

Laying down the vest with mohair yarn 'stripes'

FOUR

Hat making

Project 8: Hood shaped on a hat block

YOU WILL NEED:
minimum 100 g (3½ oz) carded wool
hood pattern (see diagram) made from a firm plastic
    such as Polyscrim, a plastic shadecloth available
    at large hardware stores and some plant nurseries
    (not the woven mesh type)
fine sheeting for a pressing cloth
soap solution
plastic squeeze-bottle to apply solution
matchstick blind
hat block

Note: Hat blocks can be enlarged or their shape altered by bandaging with crepe bandage. If you have not got a hat block, improvise—a kitchen basin bandaged into a shape works quite well. The plastic hat blocks used for making raffia hats can also be used.
Make a 25 cm (10″) sample laying down three medium layers to check the felting quality of your fleece, and the thickness.

METHOD
Place hood pattern on the blind and lay down three medium layers, overlapping the pattern by approximately 8 cm (3″) all around the top curve, but not over the bottom edge (see photograph). Neaten the bottom edge by turning the fibres back on themselves. Gently slide out the pattern and lay it on top of the pad. Pour a small quantity of soap solution onto the plastic pattern and move it to run just over the edges to mark the pattern's position on pad. Remove the pattern and wet down the pad only inside the shape of the pattern, leaving dry the 8 cm (3″) extra around the edge.

Place pattern back on wet area and pat gently to lay the fibres down and force out the air. Now, turn the dry wool back over the edges of the pattern and ease out. Fill in the bare area with three medium layers, taking the top layer over the upper curved edge to the back, reinforcing this edge so that the pattern is evenly covered with wool and only the base of the pattern can be seen.

Cover with a soft cloth and wet down the top side with soap solution. Roll up the blind over the shape

Blocked hat with the brim turned and stitched for a self edge

33

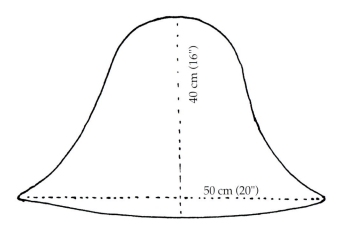

40 cm (16")

50 cm (20")

Use the grid method to enlarge the hood pattern

when you are satisfied that the thickness is even, with no thin patches.

Gently roll, adding enough solution through the blind to give you a light lather as shown in the photograph.

Examine the work frequently, and as soon as the piece holds together open the the bottom edge and turn the plastic pattern inside a half turn, to bring the edges to the middle. If a ridge has formed, gently stretch with your fingers and pat flat. Continue

rolling, and turning the pattern, until you are satisfied. If you find any thin areas, consult page 77 for repairs.

When you have an even felt that passes the tent test, full as described on page 14, rinse and roll in a towel to remove moisture.

Pull the hood over the hat block while still damp and pat and stretch into the desired shape. Tie a piece of yarn around the headline after measuring the depth of head required.

The brim is then stretched between the hands to give a flat brim (or you can use a brim block). Hold the side of one hand against the headline, and with the other hand gently stretch the brim into the position you require.

Next measure the brim to the width you require and mark with a row of pins. Cut on the line of pins, cutting towards the point of each pin and removing it away from you for accurate measurement, using the full blade of your scissors to get a smooth edge. Do not snip with the points as the end result will be ragged.

Rub the cut edges gently with your fingers, or use an emery board, to remove any rough edges.

Dry the hat before you trim it. I use a cotton grosgrain ribbon for the inside headband because it can be shrunk to fit the shape by damping with a

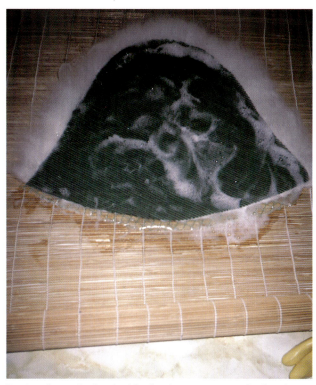

Laying down the hood with plastic pattern over the first layer of felt

Massaging the soap solution into the felt with the fingertips

little water. Synthetic ribbon will not shrink. Cut ribbon 2 cm (¾") longer than head size. Join with a 1 cm (3/8") seam. Divide ribbon and hat into four and pin headband to each quarter. Stitch in with small stitches.

Use millinery wire to shape the brim if you wish. Overcast to the edge and overlap wire a good 3 cm (1¼"). Cover with a narrow grosgrain ribbon, folded and stitched from front to back with small stitches in the ridges, slanting the needle.

The quality of the felt will determine the success of the edging. If the felt is firm, a smooth cut edge will hold the shape without the need for ribbon or millinery wire.

Self edging Turn over 1 cm (3/8") around the edge of the brim, tack, press out fullness with a damp cloth, then machine stitch a row or two. This also makes a neat edge.

Should your felt be too soft and the brim too floppy you can use a stiffener to rectify the problem. Use millinery stiffener, which is a spirit which you apply with a brush, or you can use a clear fabric stiffener which is massaged into the felt with wet hands.

PVA glue mixed with an equal quantity of water and massaged into the felt gives a firm brim. This mixture is also excellent for stiffening masks (page 40).

Project 9: 3D felting—crown extensions

Try making an eye-catching hat with extensions to the crown as shown in the photograph.

YOU WILL NEED:
250 g (8 oz) washed carded fleece
plastic hood pattern
soap solution
fabric for resists

Design and felt additions first.

Dry, rough up the edge to be attached to the crown of the hat.

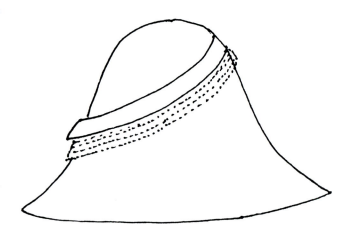

Dotted lines indicate the resist separating the addition from the hood

Cover plastic hood pattern with 2 layers of fleece, N/S, E/W as previously explained, but keep the fleece dry. Add the felted additions, with resists where they need to be separated from the crown. A few tacking stitches will help to keep them in place. Add third layer around extensions. When all is to your liking wet down over a cloth and massage gently with your fingers.

Roll in blind and check frequently to make sure the additions are felting into the hood.

Give pattern a half turn and pat out ridges or weak parts.

Lay the extensions into the second layer and wrap with cloth resist so they remain separate.

During the felting process the felt is very malleable. Some ideas
■ Draw it out, twist it, poke holes in it.
■ Lay in multicolour layers, then cut down and expose different colours.
■ Machine stitch the brim.

Felt hat with three-dimensional extensions added to the crown by the use of resists

Project 10: Hat with crown ridge

This method is suitable for a shallow-crowned country-style shade hat.

YOU WILL NEED:
250 g (8 oz) washed carded wool
soap solution
string
4 drawing pins
60 cm (24") cotton grosgrain ribbon for headband

Wrapping a crepe or elastic bandage around the block or bowl will give you the crown ridge and straight sides.

Country-style hat

Country-style felt hat with sharp crown ridge

White felt hat with soft crown ridge

METHOD

Lay down a 60 cm (24") circle or square of fleece using three medium layers according to your sample.

Felt in the usual manner, then rinse, and roll in a towel to remove moisture.

Stretch damp felt over hat block or mould and secure with a strong rubber band at headline. Ease out the fullness until all tucks have been moulded into the crown.

Tie a piece of string around the headline and adjust depth of front, sides and back of crown. If using a wooden block you can hold the crown in place with four drawing pins.

Now work on the brim, stretching and patting until it is the right shape and you can measure for an even brim with a line of pins.

Cut with full blade of scissors along the line of the pins.

Set aside to dry.

A leather trim suits this style; fine leather strips, in a wide plait of 4 to 6 ends, make a great finish.

Project 11: Beret made on a plastic ball

YOU WILL NEED:
large plastic ball approximately 60 cm (24') in
　　circumference (or larger)
100 g (3½ oz) clean carded wool or tops
small bowl about 16–18 cm (6¼"–7") in diameter
soap solution or detergent
snippets of coloured wool, silk, or yarn for decoration
1 or 2 pairs of old pantyhose

METHOD
Stand ball in the bowl to stop it rolling about and
cover with a liberal amount of soap solution. This
will hold the fleece in place.

Take a long piece of carded wool and lay it from
one edge of the bowl, over the ball, to the other edge
of the bowl. Having halved the area, take another
piece and quarter the ball. Check with diagram.

Then with shorter lengths fill in, overlapping each
strip. Pat into place. Now, taking a long length, and
starting from the top of the ball, circle the fleece
around and around until you come to the edge of
the bowl.

You now have two layers, and you can add the
decorative design in the third layer. Alternatively, you
could lay in the design on the ball before you start.
Find the way that works best for you.

Fine layers work best, alternating the direction.
Over the top gives N/S and around gives E/W. Three
layers should be sufficient, making sure you have
no thin areas.

Neaten the edge around the bowl.

Cut pantyhose according to the diagram. With the
help of another pair of hands take one leg of

*Beret made over a plastic ball, with decorative design added in
a third layer*

pantyhose and walk your hands down to the toe,
hands gathering hose in the palms.

With both pairs of hands above the ball stretch hose
over and down without displacing fleece or design.
For larger balls, you will have to use the body part of
the pantyhose. Flip the ball over and tie off pantyhose.

Repeat with the other leg, giving two nylon covers;
tie firmly.

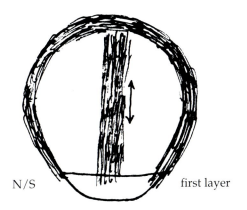

N/S and E/W layers on the plastic ball seated in the bowl

Wool laid over plastic ball before felting begins

Wet down ball with *hot* soap solution and massage gently with your hands. As the fibres settle, bounce lightly and rotate until you can see the fibres clinging to the hose.

The felting will take approximately fifteen minutes depending on the felting quality of your fleece.

Remove the top cover and note how the fibres are penetrating the remaining hose. If sufficiently felted, remove first cover. Should there be any loose pieces, continue felting by hand, otherwise remove hose and full—first in hot water, then in cold.

Wring out surplus water, place beret in towel, pat into shape, roll in towel to absorb any extra moisture. Lift beret and flop on table—this will even the shape.

Bands can be added to headline if desired, in either grosgrain ribbon or leather.

MASKS

This method can also be used to make masks, which children find great fun to do.

To add ears or other extras:

Lay down two layers, then add the ears, cut from another piece of felt, roughing up the end that will be inserted. Add extra layer, wrapping the top of insertion in cloth resist.

Any area you do not want to felt is wrapped, to prevent fibres from meshing together. The ball of felt can be pulled into shape during the fulling process, punching in the nose and working around holes for the eyes with your fingers.

Try on mask and mark position of eyes before cutting.

The edge of the fleece can be turned under and tidied before tying on the first cover.

One inventive felter I know has used a plastic bucket with the bottom removed to enable her to cover the ball by herself. She stretches the pantyhose over the bucket and removes the bucket once the ball is in position.

Koala and wombat felted masks are a delight to children to make

Project 12: Machine-sewn hats

A very smart hat can be made from a piece of felt measuring 50 cm x 64 cm (20" x 25"). I used the radiating inlay felt from the exercise on page 29.

Draw a pattern, using stiff brown paper.

Measure around the head (approximately 56 cm (22"), and decide on depth of crown, say 10 cm (4").

Cut length of paper to this measurement plus 2 cm (¾"), i.e. (56 + 2 =) 58 cm x depth of crown.

Draw an oval 15 cm x 20 cm (6" x 8") for top of crown. (Or place a wooden hat block on the paper and trace the shape—much easier!)

To make a pattern for the brim start with an oval headline, using the hat block again, and mark out the width of the brim. Cut through the centre back and fold a V shape until you get the brim shape you desire (see diagram).

Allowing a 1 cm (3/8") seam at the headline, cut out the pattern and pin together to see if the depth of the crown and the shape of the brim please you.

Make any necessary alterations to the pattern before cutting from your piece of felt.

Stitch the long piece, short ends together, placing the seam at centre back. Place pins to mark centre front and centre sides. Take oval crown piece, mark

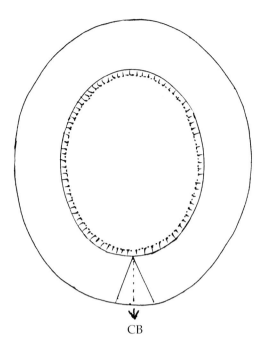

The inner circle indicates the top of the crown. The brim is shaped by the width of the V. Cut inside edge of brim, allowing turning which will be snipped at intervals and stitched to the crown

centre front, back and sides with pins and match each pin with the pins in the side piece. Try on crown to see if it is the right fit.

Sew crown and side piece together. The seam can be hidden by using invisible stitiching to join together the edges.

Method for invisible stitching

Take small stitches in a zig-zag fashion through the thickness of the felt, returning the needle in the same hole with each stitch.

Cut brim from pattern, allowing 1 cm (3/8") seam around the headline, as on the pattern.

Stitch seam in back of brim by using invisible stitching. Press with damp cloth.

Mark centre front, back and sides of brim with pins. Snip to the headline in seam allowance, every 2 cm (¾"). Place crown over snipped edge and pin in place, matching centre front, back and sides. Try on for further adjustment of design. When you are satisfied with the shape of the brim, stitch crown over the turned-up seam allowance on the headline, using a small stab stitch, which will be covered by ribbon.

Using machine stitch decoration on the brim or the crown is easy in this method of hat construction.

Machine-sewn hat decorated with a radiating inlay pattern

Project 13: Felted knitted hats

If you have ever handspun you will really enjoy making these hats. Try some blend of wool and mohair to produce a chic model.

YOU WILL NEED:
approximately 180 g (6oz) handspun or pure wool yarn
7.5 mm circular needle (UK size 1, US size 11), or set of 4 needles, giving about 7 stitches to 5 cm (2")

Using the yarn double, knit a 10 cm (4") sample square. Felt the square and record the shrinkage.

You need to measure your head, the width of the brim and the depth of the crown (see diagram) to be able to estimate the number of stitches you need to start. According to the shrinkage in your sample, you will need to add extra stitches. For example, with average head size 55 cm (22"), you would need 77 stitches. But this estimate will be very variable, depending on the degree of shrinkage in your yarn.

BASIC PATTERN (all in one piece)
Brim Using the circular needle (or set of 4 needles) and double yarn, cast on 100 stitches, approximately 7 stitches to 5 cm (2").

Because you are using the wool doubled you can try some interesting textures (e.g. one strand of wool and one of mohair). Be careful not to twist the cast-on stitches.

Join and knit 5 cm (2") in stocking stitch.

*Knit 8, k2 tog, repeat from * to the end of the row (90 stitches remain).

Knit 7.5 cm (3") for the brim width.

Next round: *k3, k2 tog, repeat from * to the end of the row (72 stitches remain) at headline.

Knit 16 cm (6¼") for the depth of the crown.

Crown
Round 1: *k2 tog, k5, repeat from * to end of the round.
Rounds 2, 4, 6: Knit.
Round 3: *k2, k2 tog, repeat from * to end of the round.
Round 5: *k2 tog, k1, repeat from * to end of the round.
Round 7, 8, 9: *k2 tog, repeat from * to end of the round.

Break off the yarn, thread through the remaining stitches and finish off.

Put hat in the washing machine, wash on a full hot cycle and cold rinse.

Place on a towel and roll out any moisture.

Felted knitted hat

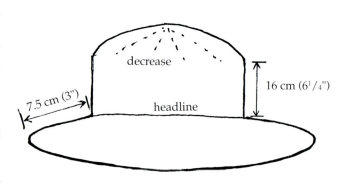

Finishing Pull the hat onto a block and ease into shape. Keep your design in mind and you can change the measurement to suit the model.

With practice you will know your yarns and be able to accurately estimate the amount of shrinkage.

Using a size larger needle, only for the brim, will give you a flatter brim.

Experiment with stitches such as moss, garter or Fair Isle on the crown.

An inner grosgrain ribbon headband will hold it in a firm shape.

FIVE

Slippers and boots

Turning your hand to making slippers and boots you can let fantasy run wild if you wish. Footwear to fit can easily be made from individual patterns.

Project 14: Moulded slippers or boots

Start the pattern by placing your foot on paper and outlining the shape of your sole. Mark a point halfway between your toe and heel. Following the diagram example, draw lines at right angles from the middle of foot and heel to the length of leg required.

Increase width at top of leg to fit calf.

Allow 3 cm(1¼″) all around for shrinkage.

Draw in any addition like an elfin toe or fancy top.

Cut this pattern from strong plastic or cardboard covered with cling wrap.

YOU WILL NEED:
200–300 g (7–8 oz) carded fleece (depends on
   length of leg)
contrast colour for decoration
zippers (optional)
leather for sole (optional)
soap solution
fine sheeting
matchstick blind

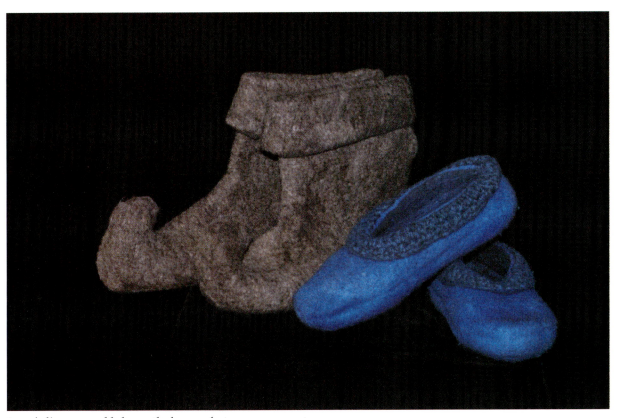

Boots and slippers moulded over the human foot

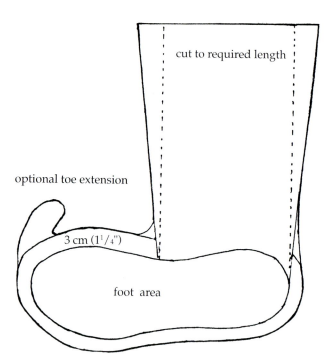

Pattern for boot or slipper—enlarge to the required size

Make a sample from your chosen fibre to obtain a strong felt (approximately three layers).

METHOD

Divide the fleece evenly so that each slipper will be the same weight.

Lay down, directly on the blind, three medium layers or as per your sample.

Place pattern on the pad, allowing 5 cm (2") of fleece to extend down sides and around the foot. Lift pattern. Add hot soap solution to centre of pad, replace pattern and pat solution out to the edge of pattern, keeping the 5 cm (2") turnover dry. Rub gently to make a firm pad.

Turn excess back over edges of leg and foot, but turn top of leg below top of pattern.

Build up three layers on this top side, wrapping last layer of leg and foot over the edge to the back. Keep the top of the pattern visible.

Cover with cloth, wet down top layer and roll in the blind. Make sure upper leg pattern is not felted over, otherwise you will have difficulty putting the slipper on!

When felt is firm, turn and felt in other direction.

Remove pattern when slipper is holding together.

You now have two options: moulding the slippers on your feet or using an old pair of sneakers to mould the feet.

You need a basin and a low stool. Another person to massage your feet is helpful.

Pull the wet felted shape gently onto your foot. Yuck! I only do one at a time.

With soapy hands massage your foot—lovely for the feet, not so good for the back. (This is where another pair of hands is useful.)

Do not be over-zealous with the hot water; remember, your foot is inside. Warm water and a good massage will reduce the size quite quickly. Do not get so carried away you forget you have to remove the slipper, or you will find you need to cut it down the side. This may not matter much for long boots, as I like the idea of a zipper in long boots, but I prefer a turnback cuff for short ones.

Finish with a good fulling and rinse.

Try the slippers on to make sure that they are not too small, and stretch to shape before drying.

Slippers made over sneakers are started by wearing the sneakers on your feet, but can be finished by holding them in your hand—this makes them easy to remove if the telephone rings in the middle of the action!

Because slippers made over sneakers turn out a loose fit I like to make a thick soft felt innner sole which I glue onto a cardboard shape. You will find this makes a very comfortable slipper.

Felt will slip on polished floors so I stitch and/or glue a soft leather to the sole. Or you can try using puffy fabric paint on the soles. Follow the manufacturer's instructions for puffing.

For a little fun, fabric paint can be used to make boots something special. See the photographs of the Four Seasons slippers on page 80—Spring, Summer, Autumn, Winter.

If you make slippers with turned-up toes, small bells attached to the toes will especially delight children.

Long zippered slippers trimmed with jester bells

Project 15: Handstitched slippers or boots

Simple slippers can be made from a flat piece of felt. Make a 25 cm (10") sample of three or four layers to obtain a strong felt.

YOU WILL NEED:
160 g (5½ oz) fleece
piece of soft leather if you prefer a leather sole
linen and embroidery threads
soap solution
matchstick blind
piece of cloth to cover the pad

METHOD
Lay down a 72 cm (28") square of three or four layers of carded fleece, placing layers at right angles to each other. Keep the thickness approximately 10 cm (4"). Cover with the cloth.

Wet down with hot soap solution and distribute moisture evenly.

Roll in the blind for two minutes, then unroll and turn under the edges.

Continue to roll until piece is firm enough to turn 90°.

Roll and turn, using the tent test to determine when the piece is ready for fulling. Full with hot then cold water.

Rub vigorously on draining board or felting board, then knead with the hands. This piece of felt needs to be well-felted to stand up to hard wear.

Rinse until all the soap is removed, roll in a towel to remove moisture and hang to dry.

Hand-stitched slippers; detail of stitching on right

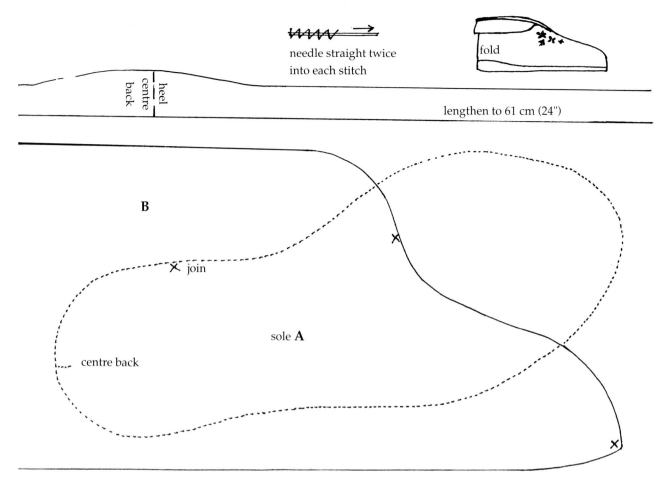

needle straight twice
into each stitch

fold

heel
centre
back

lengthen to 61 cm (24")

B

✕ join

✕

sole **A**

centre back

✕

Use this pattern as a guide to making your own personal pattern. Enlarge in photocopier to give a diagram closer to a realistic size if you're not confident about enlarging this diagram by eye or the grid method

MAKING UP

Individual slipper patterns can be made by placing your foot on paper and tracing the size. Alter the pattern diagram to suit your measurements.

Cut four pieces of sole (A). If you prefer a leather sole cut two pieces for the sole in the felt and two others in soft leather.

Place pattern B on fold and cut two. Extend length if you have increased size of the sole.

Extend length of strip to 61 cm (24") and cut one piece.

Sew bottom sole to strip using linen thread and glove stitch for strength.

Check that you have a right and left foot then sew other sole strip.

Stitch between crosses at centre front.

Now join all three thicknesses, upper strip, sole and top of slipper, leaving opening at heel to stuff sole firmly with fleece.

Should your felt be too thick for three pieces to be sewn together, eliminate the sole strip and the bottom sole. Instead add a thick inner sole to the slipper: approximately 2 mm of felt for the double sole, 4 mm for the single sole.

Embroider the cuff.

- S I X -

Small items and gifts

Small items are great fun for children to try. Encourage their imagination to flow and see what wonderful things they can create. All the items in this section can be made with simple equipment and easy felting methods. These include wrapping the piece in cloth and rolling with a rolling pin, rolling in a matchstick blind or simply dropping into a washing machine in a normal wash cycle.

Project 16: Felt balls

YOU WILL NEED:
quantity of felting fleece
snippets of coloured tops and yarns, metallic thread, etc.
pantyhose
soap solution

Remember to sample first so that you know that you are working with a good felting fleece. If you are making a number of balls and want them uniform in size weigh each quantity before starting to felt.

Small bells can be placed in the centre but you will need to wrap them in plastic cling wrap to keep them dry and prevent the wool clogging them. Two

Felt balls with colourful surface decorations. Courtesy Liz Calnan

bottletops taped together, with split peas, small beans or tiny stones inside, make inexpensive rattles.

METHOD
I like to start with a small quantity of fleece and soap and roll it in my hands until I have the size I want. Then I add the coloured tops and coloured yarn, winding them around the ball to keep a good shape.

A final soaping, then drop the ball into a pantyhose leg and tie off tightly with a piece of string. Make sure the string is secure and will not come undone during felting. Roll and squeeze by hand or use the washing machine.

You can put several balls in one leg, tying off each separately. Felt in a normal cycle in the washing machine.

After removing the balls from the pantyhose you will need to give them a final roll on the table or between the palms of your hands.

Rinse well and dry.

VARIATIONS ON BALLS
Lotus: Try 1 cm (3/8") layers of different coloured fleece or tops as you make up the ball.

After the ball has been felted and dried take a sharp knife and cut two-thirds of the way through the ball from a point you could think of as the tip of the bud. Cut again; halves, quarters, eighths and possibly sixteenths, depending on the size of the ball. Using white and graduating pinks can give you a very attractive flower, as illustrated on page 51.

Basket of fruit: Fruits such as apples, pears and bananas can be reproduced either by packing into pantyhose or moulding by hand.

Finish by painting with fabric paint applied with a small piece of foam or sponge.

Let your imagination take over and explore this method.

You would like a basket for your fruit? Cut strips of felt and weave them over and under. Stitch roughly with tacking stitches and felt only enough so you can mould the felt over a bowl and draw out a handle.

Mouthwatering felt fruits in a woven felted basket

Project 17: Stocking dolls

YOU WILL NEED:
small quantity carded fleece
wire coathanger
old pantyhose
paper for pattern

METHOD
Draw the pattern for the doll on paper.

Bend a wire coathanger to the shape in the diagram and place it in a pantyhose leg.

Trace the pattern onto the pantyhose with a laundry pen.

Machine stitch a continuous outline from the side of the head, arm, side body, legs, side body, arm and back to the side of the head, leaving an opening at the top of the head for stuffing.

Starting with the legs and using layered carded fleece, stuff the doll firmly. Laying up a square of two layers, then tearing off a strip, is the easiest way. Working with small strips helps prevent the stuffing separating into balls.

Pack down with the top of a knitting needle or a smooth piece of dowel.

Cut pantyhose from the frame and tie off tightly. Drop into a full cycle of the washing machine, then tear off the pantyhose. If any part needs reinforcement do it now: add the fleece, massage in a little soap and smooth the fibres down.

Stocking dolls—Tina and The Long Man (see page 72 also)

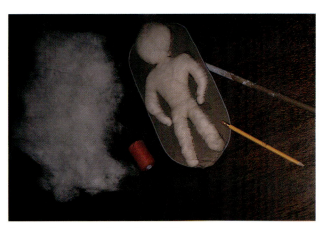

Laying down a small stocking doll

Now you have an opportunity to try out some different felts for the clothing. I recommend that you keep them fine.

Try laying in a tartan design for a skirt, using coloured wools in the top layer. Alternatively, snippets of coloured wool dropped at random in the top layer will give a confetti effect. Anchor these designs with gossamer pieces of fleece.

Plaited fleece makes great hair. Mark in the facial features with fabric paints.

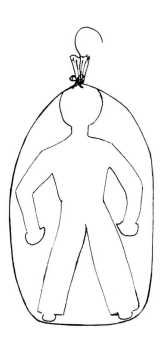

Wire coathanger with pantyhose over it and pattern drawn on

Project 18: Sculptured shapes

You can felt over solid shapes such as stones, balls and pieces of wood to make attractive door stops. Children enjoy making these.

Felting over foam rubber forms opens up a multitude of ideas. After sculpturing your foam in a simple form, wind the fleece around it until you have covered the piece entirely, remembering the N/S and E/W layers.

Put the form (now wrapped in fleece) into some pantyhose or wrap in resist material.

Lather with the soap solution and gently massage until the surface is well felted.

Rinse gently and dry. The felted form can then be painted or decorated.

Forms wrapped around pipe cleaners are made in the same way.

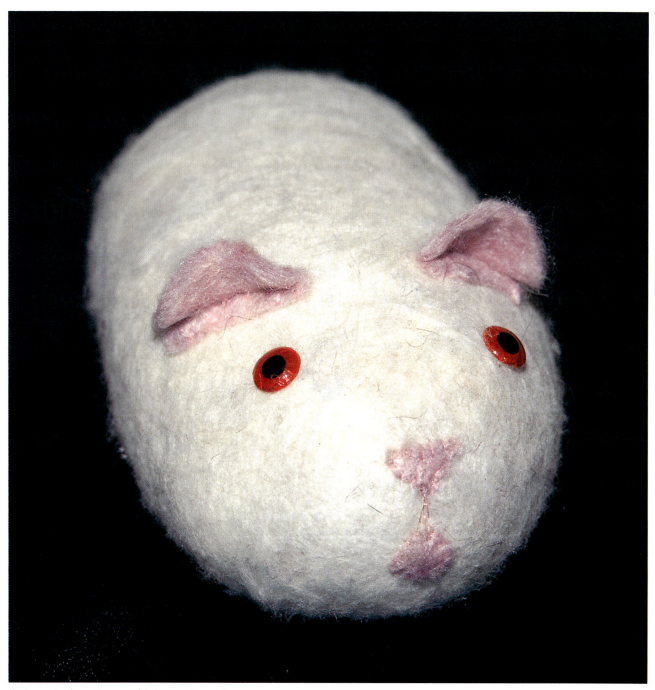

Guinea pig door stop moulded around a rock

Project 19: Using your samples

Take out your bags of 25 cm (10″) samples and offcuts from larger felting projects to make some very acceptable gifts.

If you find your samples are too small for a particular project make a patchwork piece to fit your shape. Sewing felt together is easy. Invisible stitches can be made by taking stitches back in the same hole and zigzagging the needle between the edges, drawing them together. After pressing, the seam will be flat and the stitches unseen.

SMALL PURSE

One of the quickest and easiest gift items is a small purse, made from a fine felt.

You will need a 9 cm (3½″) metal purse frame.

Cut an oval shape 15 cm x 20 cm (6″ x 8″) from a sample. Fold piece over, right sides together, and stitch each side together for 5 cm (2″) from the fold.

Attach felt with small stitches to inside of frame. Use a strong thread and gather fullness into the frame. Presto! A purse.

Small purse and spectacle case made from samples, and lotus flower made from a layered felt ball

SPECTACLE CASE WITHOUT A FRAME

Using the same technique as for the purse, lengthen the oval to 33 cm x 10 cm (13" x 4") and you have a spectacle case. Some sunglasses require a wider case, so measure up your requirements before cutting.

Choose fine felt made with fine layers; line all pieces before stitching together.

YOU WILL NEED:

felt piece 33 cm x 10 cm (13" x 4")
felt strip 2.5 cm x 40 cm (1" x 16") for the sides
felt strip 1 cm x 9 cm (3/8" x 3½") for closure
lining fabric
embroidery threads

Line each piece of felt, then make up the case, referring to the diagram. The flap is secured under the narrow strip. Embroider initials on the front for a thoughtful gift with a personalised touch.

I still use the spectacle case which I made in a felting workshop 14 years ago.

COATHANGERS

Try covering old coathangers with fine felt. For decoration, roll thin strips of felt between soapy hands, making sure they hang free from your hands. If they touch the table, the floor or your knee they will break. These can be used for bows and loops to decorate the hanger.

SEWING ACCESSORIES

Pincushions and needlebooks are great fun to make and are easy enough to be encouraging for folk of all ages venturing into the world of craft.

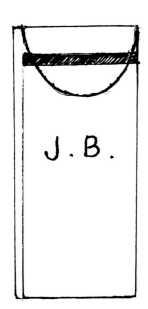

9 cm x 1 cm (3^1/$_2$" x ^{3}/$_8$")

4 cm x 9 cm (9^1/$_2$" x 3^1/$_2$")

17 cm x 9 cm (6^3/$_4$" x 3^1/$_2$")

3 cm x 43 cm (1^1/$_4$" x 17") side strip

Seamless garments

Project 20: Seamless vest

Making garments opens up lots of possibilities. Look at the vests on pages 6, 31, 55–7 and 84 for other ideas for a finished garment.

YOU WILL NEED:
approximately 500 g (16 oz) clean carded wool (tops and sheet carding make felting easier; remember fine fleece makes fine felt)
any contrast fibre or yarn
simple vest pattern
fine sheeting
soap solution
matchstick blind

First make a 25 cm (10″) sample with three medium layers and estimate shrinkage.

METHOD
Enlarge your chosen pattern to allow for shrinkage, e.g. enlarge 92 cm (36″) to 108 cm (42″). Draw the enlarged pattern on a piece of sheeting, placing the fronts to each side of the back.

Lay the cloth pattern on your matchstick blind and build up three medium layers of fleece.

Three layers should be sufficient but be guided by your sample. Garments do not need to be very thick. Softer, finer felt drapes better and is very warm. Remember to overlap each piece as you build up the

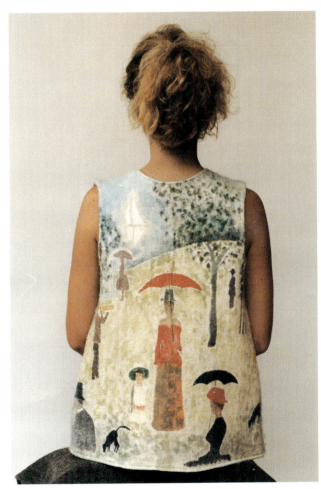

Seamless vest made in plain white wool and later painted with fabric paints

Showing back and two fronts laid together as one piece. Note dry area at top for overlapping finished shoulder seams

Laying down a seamless vest with floral surface decoration

layers and watch out for thin areas. Add decorative patterns to top surface.

LAYING IN A POCKET

After laying down two layers cut a piece of cloth the size of the required pocket plus 6 cm (2½") at top of pocket. This piece of cloth will be withdrawn after felting, leaving the pocket. Lay two medium layers over the pocket, folding over 6 cm (2½") at the top of the pocket for a smooth edge.

When laying in two pockets be very sure they balance; a few tacking stitches may help to keep them in the right position.

Cover pad with cloth, wet down with soap solution, roll up and roll gently so as not to disturb the pattern. Check to see that moisture is evenly distributed. Extra solution can be poured through the blind while rolling. If you intend felting the shoulder seams keep 12 cm (5") dry on both front and back shoulders until the body is firm enough to hold

Vest in Australian bush tones, the pattern laid in with coloured wools. Resists were used to lay in the pockets

together. Lay a piece of cloth over the back as a resist and bring both fronts over so shoulders can overlap. Make a few tacking stitches to hold the shoulders in place. Wet the shoulders with the solution and continue felting.

As soon as possible fold over and neaten the edges. When this is well done no cutting is required and the edges will be smooth.

This one piece method is wonderful for design. Small pieces of contrast colour added to the final layer can build an overall design encircling the body.

Lengthening the vest pattern will give you a jacket. Sleeves can be felted, or knitted as a feature.

FINISHING

Embroidery or appliqué can enhance your garment. Buttonhole, blanket or running stitches are very effective on felt. Glove stitch, taking the needle twice through the advancing overstitch, makes a neat edge. You could chain-stitch just in from the edge, then pick up and crochet an edging.

Try painting or stencilling a design after felting. The felt should be dry and the fabric paint not too thin, or it will soak through to the inside, making it necessary to line the garment. Fabric dyes and wool cold dyes work well. Follow the instructions for particular dyes. Set the finished design by pressing with a hot iron over a cloth. Microwaves can also be used for dyeing.

Lining your garment with silk overcomes uneven edges and gives a professional finish.

Leave a small pleat at the centre back, for felt can stretch when worn.

Buttons can be made by rolling small pieces of fleece between the hands with soap solution. Attach to garment with a shank.

Patch pockets can be sewn to the finished jacket or extra felt can be be made for sleeves. Just remember to use the same number of layers and thickness. Record method as you proceed so you can duplicate the fabric.

White wool vest finished with simple embroidery in silver Lurex thread

- E I G H T -
Felting woven cloth

Project 21: Felted woven cloth

Many simple clothing patterns can be made up in a felted woven cloth. Determine how much fabric you require, make a sample following the main instructions, and go to it.

For those who weave their own fabric, use 2/12s wool approximately 12 epi, and weave a fairly open weave.

After weaving repair any errors and machine stitch the ends to stop fraying.

Full as much as the material will take, either by hand, rubbing with hot soapy solution, or in the washing machine. Watch progress carefully to ensure that the shrinkage is even and not hard. Sampling should have given you the necessary information, but watch progress very carefully.

Rinse well to remove soap, adding a dash of vinegar to the last rinse.

Spin dry, then roll fabric onto a cardboard cylinder covered with a piece of clean cloth or plastic.

Roll and stretch to an even width. Leave to set weave and when partly dry remove and hang on the line for final drying.

If ironing is necessary iron on the wrong side. Roll back on the cylinder until you are ready to cut it out.

You will be delighted with the feel of the felted cloth.

Handwoven and felted vest

Project 22: Nuno-felt (felting onto cloth)

First the cloth is laid onto the blind and the pattern is made with the wool over the cloth. Thin down the tops by dividing into four. The thinner pieces allow for a more intricate pattern to be laid down. Only one direction of fibre is needed as you pattern with the wool. See picture below.

This technique gives a bubbled effect as the wool felts and draws up the cloth.

Unusual effects can be made by making see through areas in the felt where the cloth will bubble through, as in the picture on the right.

Sample first to see which cloth works best. I have found I get the best results with cotton gauze and cheesecloth, and other non-synthetic openweave cloths.

A soft cotton or silk chiffon with a wool and silk blend tops can look exquisite for a stole or blouse.

To make soft flower petals or felt for card inserts try laying down very fine layers on a piece of woollen material. After lightly felting, the piece can be peeled off the backing and will be fine and even.

Wall hangings and pictures are quite successful felted onto light material. Resists can be used, so they can be withdrawn after felting and the area can be padded to give a 3D effect (see page 59).

Nuno-felt vest with free-form edges. Courtesy Joyce Darley

Felting onto cotton gauze. The felted leaves were added later

Project 23: Chiffon-backed stole

YOU WILL NEED:
1.5 m (1¾ yds) silk or cotton chiffon (makes two
   stoles)
100 g (3½ oz) fine carded Merino wool
fine sheeting
soap solution or detergent
matchstick blind

First make a sample following the main instructions
and estimate shrinkage.

METHOD
Divide the chiffon lengthwise into two pieces 150 cm
x 50 cm (60″ x 20″).

Lay down matchstick blind with the chiffon
directly on it, then two fine layers of fleece at right
angles to each other (N/S and E/W).

With your fingers make 3 cm (1¼″) holes in the
fleece, circling to give the holes smooth edges. You
could make holes all over, or just a few at each end.
The holes could form a pattern, measured carefully
so the pattern is balanced.

If the stole is too long for your work area, lay half
and roll the blind. As you roll the blind, move down
the table and lay the rest of the stole and the pattern.

Roll up the blind and secure with three rubber
bands, one at the middle and one either end.

Try cold felting for this project. Mix detergent with
one-third bucket of water. Stand the blind in the
bucket and ladle water over the blind and in the end.
Lift the blind onto the table and roll gently for
approximately five minutes.

Unroll the blind, check and neaten edges.

Reroll and continue for another five minutes. Dry
off the liquid if there is too much water. Unroll and
turn the piece 90°, folding sides in half to fit, and
inserting resists to prevent the felt adhering to itself.

Continue rolling until you have the required
degree of felting. You will find the chiffon has
gathered as the wool has shrunk. Little bubbles of
cloth will rise from the holes.

Full in hot then cold water and hang to dry.

Chiffon-backed stole

- N I N E -

Group projects

Project 24: 3D wall-hanging

YOU WILL NEED:

quantity of good felting fleece for background

good collection of various colours

two pieces of sheeting a little larger than the size of
the picture

laundry pen to mark out the design

piece of plate glass or picture-framing glass approx.
36 cm (14") square to press the fibres into place

soap solution

matchstick blind

METHOD

Once you've decided on a picture you want to felt, you'll have to draw up a pattern. You may need to enlarge the picture you've chosen by the grid method, e.g. 1 cm enlarged to 5 cm (or ½" to 2½"). Place tracing paper over the picture, trace the picture, then draw 1 cm (½") squares over picture.

On butcher's paper or art paper draw the same number of 5 cm (2½") squares.

Trace picture for Ned Kelly wall-hanging

The first details laid down

Second layer of detail in place

Laying in the resists

Adding the backing layers

Copy each line within each square into the same position in the enlarged square. Paint the colours you are going to use on this enlarged picture.

Tape the picture to a window and tape a piece of soft sheeting over it. With the laundry pen trace the basic design onto the cloth. (Small details can be added when felting if you keep the painted picture in front of you.)

Using the method I describe here, you will be laying in the detail first, and finishing with the background. This means the picture will come out as a mirror image of the original. If you want it the same way round, reverse the cloth and tape it to the window again and go over the lines from the other side.

Place cloth with the clearly marked design on the blind.

Select the colours you are going to use. Just like mixing with paints, wools can be blended to give you an exact shade. For example, tree trunks can be creatively represented using brown, yellow, pink and grey. The colours can be softened by carding with a

The finished picture

little bit of white wool. Blue wool carded with red will give a purple colour.

If you do not have a carder, use a comb or just cut some fibres and mix together.

If you are working with a group on a large project, one person can be nominated to blend the colours. Divide up the carded wool and give each person an area to work on. (For this sort of group project, six is probably the maximum workable number.)

Hang your colour guide where all the group can refer to it. As you work through the design you will need to keep an eye on the picture or you will lose your way.

Having selected your colours start from the foreground of the picture and work down through the depth, finishing with the furthest part (e.g. the horizon or sky). In the Ned Kelly example, Ned was done first, followed by the trees and lastly the far distant sky.

Fine detail can be laid down in any direction, with large areas kept to N/S, E/W layers. For very fine detail, dampening the fibres with wet fingers and

Ned Kelly—the figure in the hanging is about 18 cm (7") tall, twice the size of this sketch

Detail of one corner of Ned Kelly picture

placing a piece of glass on top will set the lines.

Use scissors to cut sharp lines to give detail. Fine lines can be created by rolling wisps of fleece between the hands.

Leaves and foliage are snippets of cut wool. The technique is similar to making wool pictures. Birds can be tiny V-shapes in the sky.

Remember where you place the light—keep it coming from the one direction with, of course, shaded areas on the other sides of objects.

When you are satisfied the detail has been laid down, reinforce the areas you want to lift into 3D. Cut these pieces from another piece of sheeting, tracing the shapes from the original picture. Lay these pieces onto the selected places. They should be bold and not too small. Make sure the lines are simple since you need to be able to get into them with a knitting needle and stuff them.

When you are satisfied with the picture, that the laying down is even and the resists are in place, cover with two medium layers of backing fleece, going N/S and E/W. Remember that some of this colour will work through so select a blue or grey that will enhance the overall picture.

Cover with another piece of sheeting. If you are working alone, damp sheeting is easier to flip out and over the pad.

Wet down with hot soap solution and pat the moisture out to the edges.

Roll gently in the blind, remembering not to distort the pad when rolling.

When the moisture is even and there are no dry patches, turn the edges to the top (which is the back of the picture). Work the felt until a nice lather appears. Ease out any creases.

When the piece is firm turn 90°, remove the pattern cloth and give it a final roll. Watch the pattern and roll to bring proportion to the finished picture, remembering that felt shrinks in the direction of the rolling. Pictures only need light felting otherwise distortion will occur.

When satisfied, full, first in hot, then cold water.

Place on a towel and roll out any surplus moisture. Dry with a row of pegs holding the top of the picture.

When the picture is completely dry, make a very small incision, approximately 1 cm (3/8") in the centre of each area to be padded.

With the top of a knitting needle, stuff over the resist with very small amounts of matching stuffing. Leaving the resists in prevents the felt from stretching and also prevents the needle weakening the surface.

Stuff evenly then sew up the slit, which will by now have increased in size. Use invisible stitches.

Press these areas lightly.

Make a long strip of felt about 2.5 cm (1") finished width. Sew loops cut from this strip to the top and bottom of the picture to take the hanging rods.

Stand back and enjoy.

Project 25: Gunya (personal sun shelter)

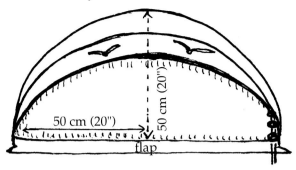

YOU WILL NEED:

250 g (16 oz) white felting fleece
large piece of sheeting to take the design
white paper
laundry pen to mark out designs
4.5 m (5 yds) 1.57 mm wire (gauge similar to
   coathanger wire)
4.5 m (5 yds) 5 mm (¼") plastic tube
clear plastic wrap
broom handle, or 120 cm (48") heavy dowel
small quantity coloured wool
soap solution
large matchstick blind

METHOD

Draw the pattern onto the sheeting with the laundry pen, enlarging by a factor of 10 (1 cm = 10 cm; ½" = 5"). Draw any decorative motifs on white paper.

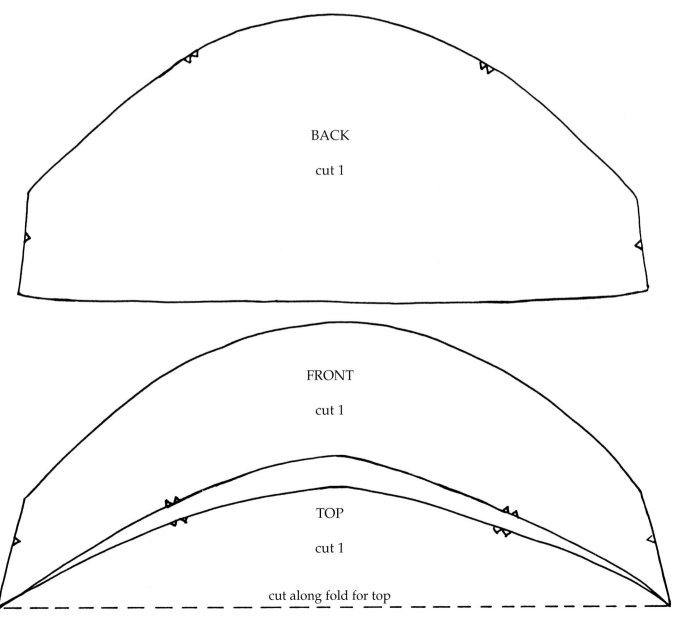

BACK

cut 1

FRONT

cut 1

TOP

cut 1

cut along fold for top

Front and back views of the gunya

Laying down the gunya

Cover motifs with a piece of clear plastic wrap and build up two fine layers of coloured fleece, patting down with wet fingers to lay the fibres.

At the same time other members of the group can be laying two medium layers, N/S and E/W, over the main pattern pieces.

Next, position the motifs on the main pattern pieces, adding any further decorations required.

Cover with pieces of cloth and wet down. Roll up and felt in the usual way with a hot soap solution.

Turn edges in and remove the top cloth after about five minutes rolling and when the pad is beginning to hold together. Roll until firm.

Turn 90° and roll in the other direction, keeping an eye on the pattern pieces to see that they retain their shapes, rolling until the pieces pass the tent test.

Full in hot then cold water.

Roll in a towel and remove excess water.

When pieces are dry give a light press if necessary.

Pin two top seams, overlapping by 2 cm (¾″), and stitch on both edges to give a flat seam.

Join short side seams.

The back extension can then be sewn in place with the same flat seam overlapped 2 cm (¾″).

Cut three pieces of wire each 150 cm (60″) long, and turn one end back 4 cm (1½″) so that it will thread through the seam without catching.

Cover the wire lengths with the plastic tubing.

Insert the three pieces of covered wire through the three flat seams.

Cut the broom handle or dowel to make two pegs each 60 cm (24″) long. Taper one end of each peg. With a pair of pliers shape one end of each plastic covered wire to go around a peg and twist approximately three turns. Make sure the sharp ends of the wire are covered by the plastic tubing.

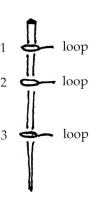

Having placed the wires over one peg, measure the length to the other peg, as adjustments may need to be made to the lengths of the wires.

Slide the pegs through the top front loop of the gunya first, then the top and finally the base. The top of the peg inside the dome will give good support.

Drive the two wooden pegs into the sand until the back flap can be covered with sand to help keep out draughts and steady the structure.

To collapse, remove pegs, shake gunya free of sand and fold. You can keep it in a specially made carry bag or an ordinary pillowcase big enough to take the gunya, the pegs, a small cushion and a book. Your comfort in the sun is assured.

Placing the motifs

Carry bag

YOU WILL NEED:
piece of calico 140 cm x 40 cm (55" x 16")
120 cm (48") cord for drawstring

Machine 3 cm (1¼") hem on short ends, turning under raw edges. Machine the side seams to fold of hems.

Place drawstring in the slots and knot the ends.

Finished gunya on the beach, showing back flap buried in the sand to anchor it

Project 26: Inlay blanket

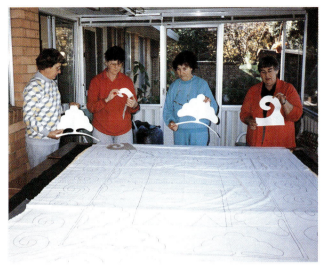

The pattern cloth for the inlay blanket; demonstrating the templates

Laying in the surface patterns

Laying-in almost complete

Making the backing layer that will cover the pattern

Spirals of wool prepared for pattern on back of rug

Laying in spirals in random order after the backing layer was placed over the front pattern

Rolling up the blind (with extreme care)

Release of tension in a felting dance!

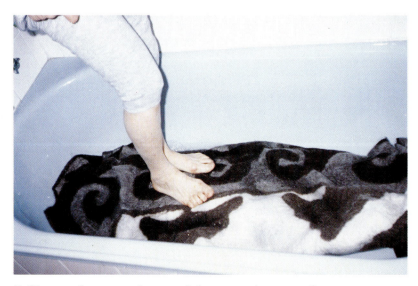

Fulling—perhaps not quite as much fun as pressing grapes (but not as messy, either!)

Pressing the fibres flat with a giant 'rolling pin' —a piece of plastic agricultural pipe

The finished blanket—a result to be proud of

- T E N -

Challenges

The items in this book are graded according to difficulty. When you feel confident with flat felting you will natually progress to a beret or hat. A time will come, however, when you really need to take felting to its limits.

Picture making in three dimensions, as described on pages 59–62, can be an interesting challenge. The areas you can raise with resists include trunks of trees, rocks, human and animal bodies, fence-rails, flowers—it just depends on the picture. As you get more more experienced you can become more adventurous.

The shapes for the areas to be stuffed are cut from calico and laid in the middle layer. Mark all resists with a tacking thread so you don't lose them!

After felting, fulling and drying cut a small opening at the back where the resist can be drawn out easily.

These areas can be gently stuffed using the end of a knitting needle. It is preferable to use the same fleece as the surface colour. Sew up the slit invisibly, passing stitches through the thickness of felt.

Some thought needs to be given to the design so that you gently pull out the resist on a straight path so it can free itself.

For example, bushranger Ned Kelly (page 61) was lifted from the background by cutting a resist body shape, and after felting and drying, withdrawing it from a small slit at the back of the work. Stuffing this area made it stand out and accentuate and dominate the picture.

A heading to take a hanging rod can be felted in by placing a piece of material across the top. When felted, this will be removed to take the rod.

Preserving felt pictures

Moths and silverfish love felt. Felt hangings should be treated with a mothproofing solution added to the rinsing water or by spraying hangings with a low irritant insect spray. A dash of eucalyptus oil in the rinse water is an effective moth deterrent.

Project 27: Kangaroo

YOU WILL NEED:
woollen material or blanket for backing (not too old or 'shrinkability' will be poor)
carded fleece
soap solution
butcher's paper
pattern of kangaroo—5 pieces
matchstick blind
wool for stuffing

Cut a 25 cm (10") square from the woollen material to make a sample. Raise the pile by brushing with a wire brush. This helps the bonding. Felt three medium layers onto the material. The backing should be puckered and firmly attached.

Matilda and her Joey

METHOD

Enlarge the kangaroo pattern to the size you require and trace onto backing fabric, making sure you have left and right sides of head, body, legs, tail and joey. Lay two or three medium layers, depending on sample, following the pattern outlines on the backing fabric.

Wet down with soap solution, roll up in the blind, and felt until the fleece is bonded with the fabric.

Full and dry.

Cut out pattern allowing 1 cm (3/8") seams. Machine pieces together, leaving an opening along the back. Stuff the tail, head and feet, then the body until very firm. Stuff the joey, embroider its eyes and nose, and position in pouch. Sew up firmly.

Stitch on kangaroo's ears and embroider eyes and nose.

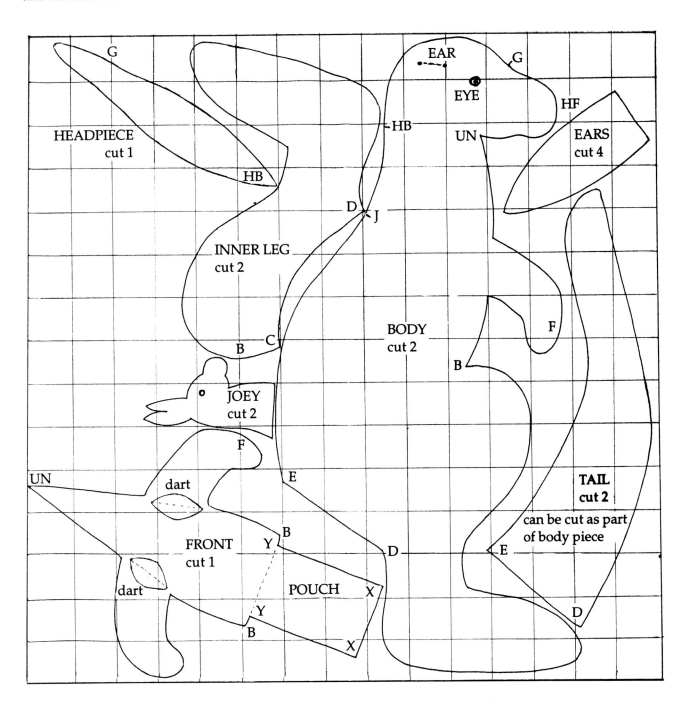

Join tail to body. Fold X to Y for pouch. Join top of leg D–C. Join body piece B–D. Sew darts on front. Stitch in from UN to B. Catch along top of pouch. Set in headpiece. Sew ears together.

Project 28: Wombat

YOU WILL NEED:

wombat pattern, enlarged to the size you require
quantity of grey wool
1 m (1¼ yds) woollen material, preferably with good
   pile
wool for stuffing
two eyes and a nose (available from craft
   departments) in size to suit
crepe or elastic bandages
needle and thread

METHOD

This wombat was made from a woollen material with
a good pile, stuffed with fleece until moderately firm.

Two medium layers of fleece were laid at right
angles (E/W and N/S) around the whole animal,
tacked in place where necessary.

The whole wombat was bandaged with an elastic
bandage (a crepe bandage could be used instead) so
that there would be no slipping during felting. A few
more tacking stitches keep everything together.

Soap solution was added liberally and the wombat
given a good shampoo. (Just like washing the dog!)

When you feel that the fleece is bonding remove
bandages and continue until felt has firmly attached
to the woollen material.

If you find some bare patches dry off those areas
with a towel. Brush up the pile, add a little extra fleece
and continue the felting.

The ears were felted and shaped first and laid into
the first layer. Alternatively, they could be stitched to
the animal before felting.

This is not the quickest method of felting but it is
a great experiment and good fun.

In a variation of this technique, Long Man on page
49 was felted in pantyhose, then brightly coloured
fleece was wound around to represent skin, jacket
and trousers and felted onto the shape. Tearing away
the pantyhose leaves long fibres that help bind the
overfelting, or you can rough up the surface so the
new fibres can bind.

I expect that quite a number of old felt or woollen
toys could be rejuvenated by brushing up a pile and
over-felting with some bright colours.

An irresistible wombat, over-felted on a stuffed wool fabric body

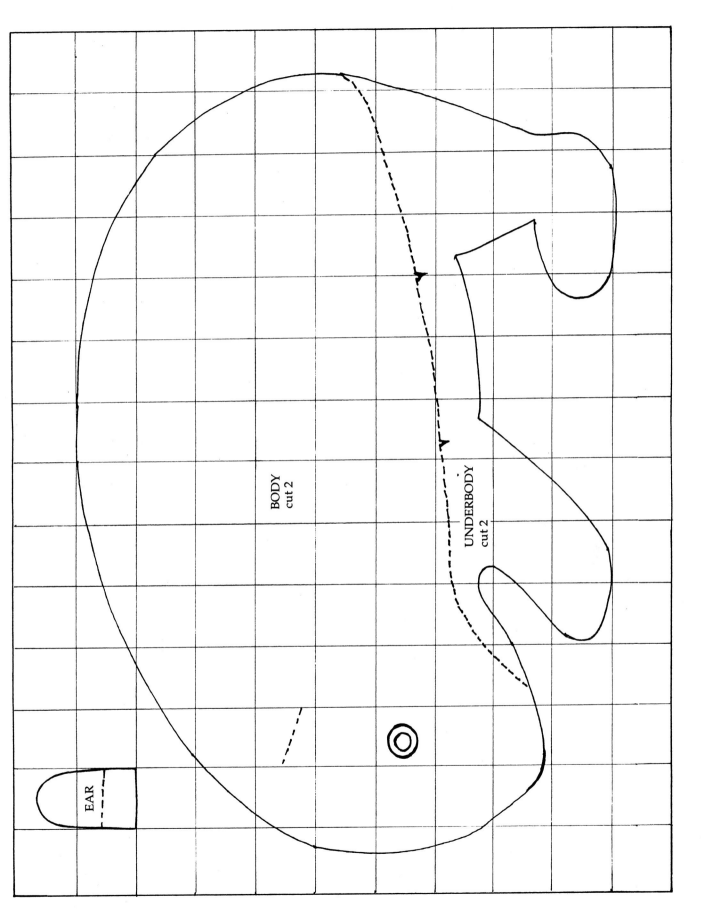

BODY
cut 2

UNDERBODY
cut 2

EAR

Project 29: Emu

Heckles the Emu

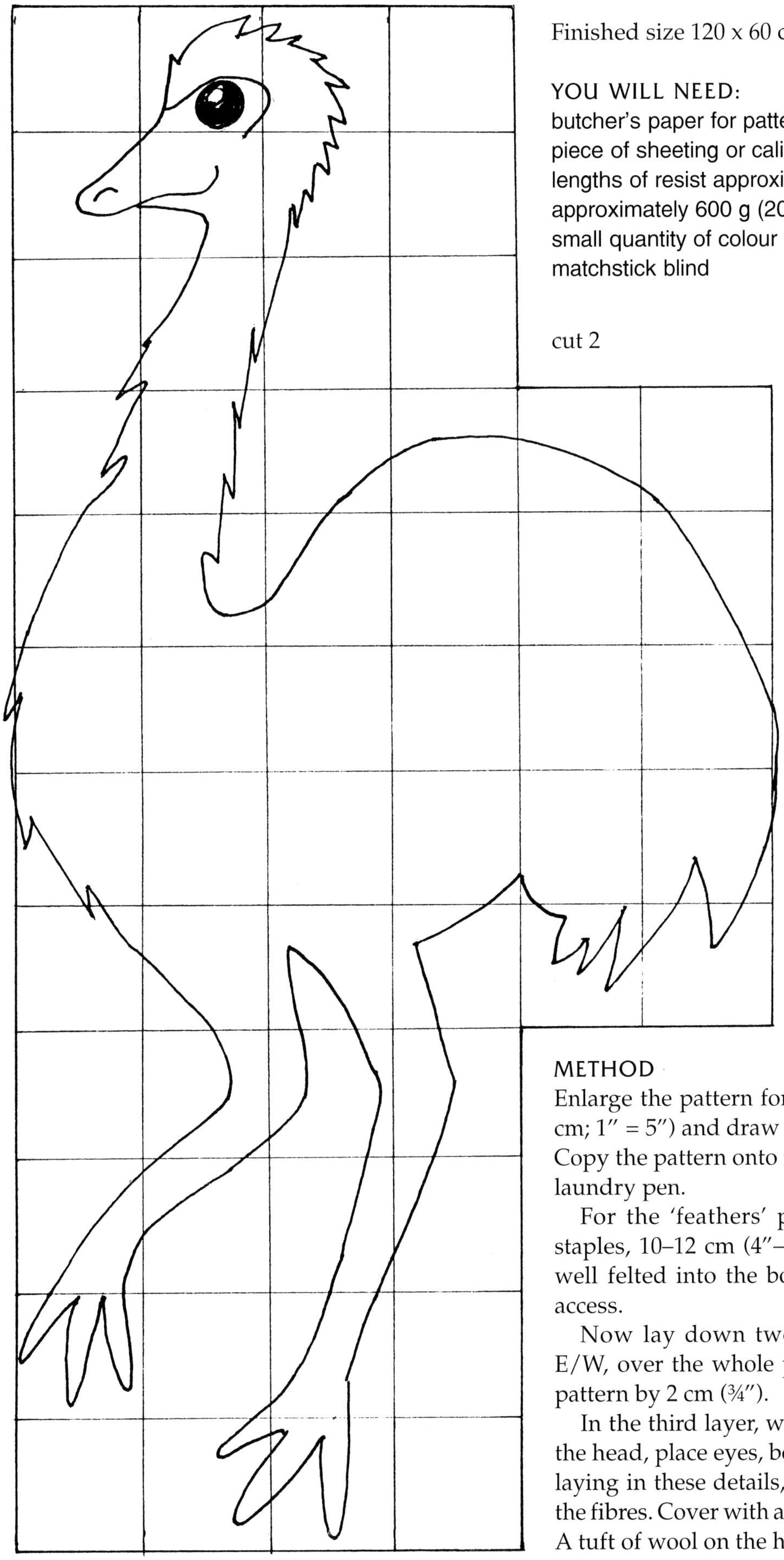

Finished size 120 x 60 cm (48" x 24")

YOU WILL NEED:
butcher's paper for pattern
piece of sheeting or calico
lengths of resist approximately 10 cm (4") wide
approximately 600 g (20 oz) grey fleece
small quantity of colour for eyes and features
matchstick blind

cut 2

METHOD

Enlarge the pattern for the emu by 5 (2.25 cm = 10 cm; 1" = 5") and draw it out on the butcher's paper. Copy the pattern onto the piece of sheeting with the laundry pen.

For the 'feathers' pull out a quantity of good staples, 10–12 cm (4"–5") long so that they will be well felted into the body. Set them aside for easy access.

Now lay down two medium layers, N/S and E/W, over the whole pattern, just overlapping the pattern by 2 cm (¾").

In the third layer, which will run N/S, start with the head, place eyes, beak and other features. When laying in these details, dampen the fleece to flatten the fibres. Cover with a piece of glass to set the detail. A tuft of wool on the head gives a comical touch.

One-third of the length of the staple should be inside the layers.

Work down the neck, placing in some shorter, lighter-coloured staples until the body is reached, then longer and darker staples look better. Each row needs a resist placed around the hanging staples; the rows *must* be kept separate, otherwise the 'feathers' will felt together. Seven or eight rows of staples should be sufficient.

The legs are plain. Separate with a cloth to prevent them felting together.

Cover with a damp cloth.

You now have, from bottom to top: matchstick blind + cloth pattern + three layers of fleece, with one-third the length of the inserts in the top layer, covered with a damp cloth.

Lightly press with a hot iron to lay the fibres. Add soap solution, distribute over the whole pattern. Pat down with felting tool to distribute moisture.

Roll gently in the blind and continue the felting process until firm enough to turn 90° and felt in the other direction.

Turn in edges and continue felting until firm. Full gently and dry.

Felt a mirror image of the body so you have a right and left side.

After the two sides are dry, place the two pieces right sides together and sew strongly close to the edge. Leave an opening approximately 15 cm (6") long under the tail for stuffing.

Turn right side out and free any caught staples from the seam.

Stuff head *firmly*, then the neck, the legs and lastly the body.

Emu before felting—some of the resists between the layers of feathers are just visible

This animal will be too heavy to stand on its legs but makes a great talking point or a cuddly toy for a favourite child.

I have also made an emu by laying the detail directly onto the pattern, then adding the two final layers. The benefit of this method is that you can wet in the eyes and beak directly onto the pattern piece. Follow the method you prefer.

Detail of emu body

ELEVEN

Troubleshooting

1. Spongy felt

1. Fleece comes either from an old sheep or from a breed that does not felt well.
2. The water may be too hard—try adding one teaspoon of ammonia or one teaspoon of water softener to the solution.
3. The fleece may have been treated with a shrinkproof treatment (unusual, but it does happen). Even using an electric sander will not make such a fleece hard and firm.

Remember all felting attempts will find a use. Spongy felt makes great inner-soles for shoes. You can strengthen it by quilting to make a comfortable base for seat covers.

2. Fibres slipping, refusing to felt

1. Too much water, so the fibres are floating.
2. Too much soap, making the fibres slip and slide instead of gripping.

3. Small bubbles in the felt

This sometimes occurs when felting a crossbreed fleece. You can see the fibres curling instead of being smooth as in a Merino fleece.

This can be used as an advantage in design, especially when used as a contrast to smooth felt.

All the above problems can be eliminated if you sample first and get to know the character of the fleece.

4. Creases in the felt

1. You may not be checking on your progress. Look frequently so you can ease out creases as you go. Stretch the piece between the fingers and pat down—the ridge or crease will flatten.
2. The blind may be rolled too tightly before the fibre starts to felt, causing the fleece to be pushed ahead of the roll and creasing. Roll less tightly.

3. Wetting down may be uneven. Wet down over a cloth. This helps to disperse the water evenly and you can pat down the mass, or lightly press, before you roll.

5. Thin areas

1. Can be caused by uneven laying down and not overlapping wool correctly.
2. Handling the piece too roughly before fibres mat together can create thin areas.
3. Not overlapping correctly around the edge of a resist can also cause thin areas. Do not panic! Dry off the thin area with a towel, rough up the pile, add extra fleece and felt over. Very often simply pushing a thin area in on itself and rolling or massaging it will be sufficient to rectify the problem; the addition of extra fleece may not be necessary.

Electric sanders can be useful to join pieces together, as in seams or hole mending.

Dry the surfaces to be joined and brush up the pile (a wire brush is handy for this). Bring the surfaces together, cover with a cloth, add a little soap solution and vibrate with the sander. This hastens the procedure of joining the pieces together.

6. Contaminated felt

1. White flecks: The lacing string in the blind is wearing. Lay a piece of cloth over the blind before putting down the pad. (Time for a new blind!)
2. Mysterious bits of coloured fleece: Always hose the blind after use and pick off any pieces of fleece from previous felting. Washing off excess soap also prolongs the life of the blind.
3. Grass seeds: It is better not to use dirty fleece in the first place, but if a few grass seeds do turn up in your felt, remove them with tweezers when the felt is dry.

7. Refuses to felt

Try another fleece.

8. Moths

For wall hangings and other ornamental felt pieces, moth-proofing is essential.

Perigan Moth-Proofer, available from Kraft Kolour (see suppliers list, page 94), is a very good product. Follow the instructions on the container.

Small items can be treated with any good household insect spray but this will not have a lasting effect.

See also Appendix 1: How and why wool fibres felt (page 86).

Gallery

Sleeveless jacket by Joyce Darley

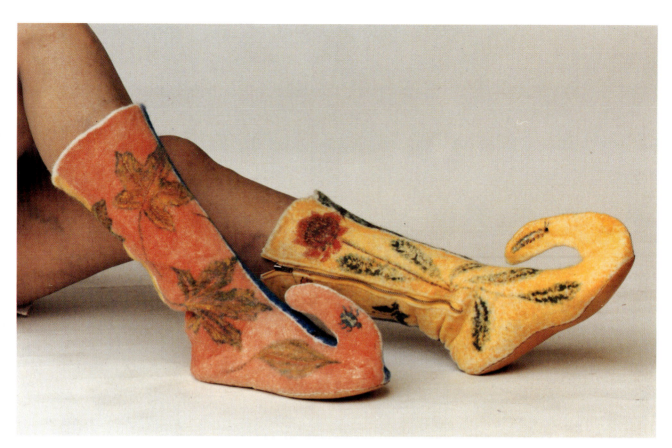

Four Seasons boots, fabric paint on finished felt, by Joan Fisher

Wall hanging by Liz Calnan

'Reflections at Twilight, Yeoval Creek': wall-hanging by Joan Fisher

'Fisher's Ghost': wall-hanging by Joan Fisher

Jointed teddy bear with hand-embroidered paws by Joan Fisher

Wearable art by Christine Sloan—capes and dresses in fine felting

Collection of handbags by Liz Calnan

Australian Flowers by Joyce Darley

Dream Fragment III and detail by Carol Divall

Outback hat and vest by Joan Fisher

Mushrooms and elf by Joan Fisher

Child's skirt in nuno-felt by Joan Fisher

How and why wool fibres felt

JENNY HOPPER

To understand how and why wool fibres felt, it is important to know about the relevant aspects of the structure of wool fibres and how they behave during the felting process.

Structure of wool fibres

Length and fineness
Wool fibres in their natural form can vary in length and diameter according to the breed of sheep, the condition of the sheep and the length of time since the sheep was last shorn. Most wool fibres range in length from 5 cm to 30 cm (2" to 12") and in diameter from 14 microns (0.014 mm) to 45 microns (0.045 mm).

Crimp
The fibres are even (regular) in diameter and are also crimped or waved along the length. The number of crimps (waves) per centimetre increases with the fineness of the fibre, so the lower the micron count of the wool the greater the number of crimps per centimetre along the fibre length. The importance of wool crimp in felting is that fine fibres (i.e. with many crimps) tend to overlap the other fibres placed near them when the fibres are spread out for felting, ensuring that the finished felt will be light and fine and very strong because the fibres have entangled where the crimps overlapped.

Scales
The surface of wool fibres is formed from overlapping epithelial cells or scales, pointing from the root to the tip of the fibre and creating a serrated surface. These scales can only be seen with magnification, but by running your finger and thumb along the length of a single fibre in one direction and then back in the other direction, you will be able to determine which is the root and which is the tip end of the fibre. The movement towards the tip will be smoother than in the other direction, because you have been 'closing' the overlapping scales as your fingers moved from the root towards the tip of the fibre. Movement in the other direction is rough in comparison, meaning you were 'opening up' the scales from the tip towards the root.

Directional frictional effect (DFE)
If you place a few moist wool fibres (all with their tips at the same end) on the palm of one hand and gently rub them back and forth along the length of the fibres with the fingers of the other hand you will find that they all migrate in the one direction on your hand—towards the root end. This is because there is less resistance to movement in that direction. This ability of wet wool fibres to move in a rootward direction when agitated is known as the directional frictional effect (DFE). In fact the root end of the fibre curls around itself. In the felting process as the fibres curl around their root ends they entangle with other curling fibres nearby, thus reducing the overall size of the fabric and causing shrinkage to occur.

Effect of heat and acid or alkali
Heat and the presence of an acid or alkali contribute to the felting process. Fibres become more flexible, more swollen and more likely to move and distort and entangle with other fibres when heated. Alkaline or acidic conditions also encourage the swelling of the fibres, leading to greater inter-fibre contact and inter-fibre friction.

The felting process

Felting is the irreversible shrinkage of fabric formed of wool fibres. It is achieved by agitating the fibres while they are wet, and is enhanced by heat and the presence of alkali in the form of washing soap (it is easier to use soap, which is a mild alkali, than to use acid, for felting by hand). Wool fibres felt because they are crimped (which encourages overlapping and later entanglement) and have scales (which results in the directional frictional effect, i.e. the fibres curling at the root end).

Finer wool fibres are more successful for fine, strong felt because finer fibres have more crimp, allowing for overlapping and later entanglement, and because the fine fibres are dense within the felt, providing more scales and enabling the DFE to effectively create strength through maximum entanglement and shrinkage.

Coarser wool fibres are more successful for thicker strong felt, because with less crimp many more fibres are needed, thus creating a thicker mass of entangled fibres. Coarse fibres usually need more agitation in the felting process to maximise this entanglement.

Felting with other hair fibres

All animal fibres with a scale structure can be felted because DFE can occur to some extent in all of them. However, wool is by far the easiest and most successful fibre to felt because its scales overlap very closely along the fibre length. Alpaca, mohair, cashmere, cashgora and camel-down fibres all have scales but they are spaced much further apart along the fibre length than wool's scales. Consequently DFE is not as effective, and because these fibres lack crimp, permanent entanglement of the fibres is not as good. While the finished felt can be soft, it is usually possible to easily pull fibres out of the felt, and so greater effort needs to be made to agitate the fibres during felting. The presence of 'guard fibres' is a problem, as these will not felt because they have virtually no scale structure, are thicker and not very flexible.

Alpaca, mohair, cashmere, cashgora and camel-down can be more successfully felted when blended with at least 50% wool fibres. Angora rabbit fibre has traditionally been used for felted hats but this has been done mainly with a pressure and steaming process difficult to reproduce for hand felting. Angora fibres are more truly a hair, like human hair, with few scales and no crimp, and are best felted when blended with a high percentage of wool.

Why some wools fail to felt

1. Some wool fibres in tops form have been treated to make them 'machine washable', i.e. shrinkage is controlled. The wool fibres have been minutely coated with chemicals to prevent the scales from acting normally under conditions of heat, moisture, agitation and alkalinity for DFE to occur. Always check when purchasing wool tops to ensure if this or other 'machine washable' treatments have been used.

2. Sometimes unlabelled sliver and tops, which appear to be 100% wool, are in fact blends of wool and nylon (or other synthetics), which are useful to spinners who can produce yarns and garments in which shrinkage is controlled. Such blends will not produce good quality felt, because the synthetic fibres lack the necessary structure and they will not felt in. Always check the fibre content before buying unlabelled sliver or tops.

3. Wool which has been stored in unwashed staple form for a long time under poor conditions (in someone's back shed with large changes in temperature and humidity over the years!) may have started degrading, e.g. breakdown of the scales has commenced, preventing them from functioning normally during the felting process. Always check by sampling the ability of the wool to felt.

References
Gohl, E.P.G. and Vilensky, L.D. *Textile Science*, Longman Cheshire, Melbourne 1983
Fritz, Anne and Cant, Jennifer *Consumer Textiles*, Oxford University Press, Melbourne 1986

Teaching felting

The day will come when you are proficient in the craft of felting and will wish to pass on your knowledge to others. Perhaps you are already a teacher, and you can see the possibilities of including felting in your school programme.

There is scope within the NSW Department of School Education's Textile and Design Syllabus 7–10 (refer to pages 7 to 19) to include felting. A felting course could teach:

the properties of fibres and felting
history of felting and cultural 'influences'
skills in designing felted fabrics and constructing
 garments
evaluating felted structures and design
some advantages in non-woven fabrics

1. Felting provides opportunity for a creative and satisfying leisure activity.
2. Felting provides pride and positive self-concept through individual and group achievements.
3. Through felting students have the opportunity to assess the quality of their designs and construction of felted garments and textile items.
4. Felting is a process which uses fibres without waste or processing—environmentally friendly.
5. Felting is used for many clothing items and textile arts. It is used in many cultures.

Jenny Hopper's explanation of how and why wool fibres felt (Appendix 1) will be of great assistance to Science teachers and indeed to all who want to understand the amazing structure of wool. Understanding the felting process will give you new insights into all the possibilities of felting.

The addition of threads, natural fibres and materials opens the mind to exciting experiments in texture such as collage, overlays, padding, slashing, embroidery and many more innovations. As in all teaching a few good samples of artistic felting will inspire the student to explore many methods of making exciting pieces.

From a good supplier buy a quantity of coloured tops that are suitable for felting (e.g. Merino).

Introduce felting by making small items. For example, make a square of felt to show the student how to blend colours and add texture. This can be achieved by introducing threads, other wool, small pieces of woollen or silk cloth and the like to the basic square being felted.

Remember that synthetic fibres do not felt into the fibres; if you use them, they have to be anchored by the wool. This knowledge can add another dimension to decoration, in that even tiny mirrors (*shisha*, found in some items of Indian origin) can be added if they are held in place with felt surrounds.

Stitching and embroidery is another option that can be used in conjunction with felting and has the benefit of utilising another skill with the felting process.

YOU WILL NEED:
plastic for covering work tables
absorbent cloth for wiping up extra moisture
towel to dry the hands and for rolling the finished felt
soap solution (see page 12)
ice-cream container or small bowl for mixing
wool tops
decorative yarns

Do not have the students start until the method has been demonstrated and everyone is familiar with the process. Demonstrate, and emphasise that you do not need to use a lot of water. Beginning students usually use too much water and not only float the fibres but also flood the floor!

Analyse the students' work so that everyone can benefit from the mistakes and successes.

Felting is wonderful for bringing out individual expression. Manipulating a natural product and getting such quick results is very satisfying.

Finished squares can be used to make a variety of small items; if they are very thin they can be used in greeting cards or as bookmarks.

Medium thickness pieces can be used as patchwork. Here the possibilities and opportunities for creativity are endless. The felt squares can be cut, rearranged on a felt backing, stitched, glued or decorated, made into a wearable item, a toy, a picture or a bag to name but a few suggestions.

Cutting the surface of thick felt made from different coloured layers will reveal the layered colours. Use sharp scissors or a blade.

Glossary

Batt A piece of layered carded wool

Carding A process of opening up the fibre, removing foreign matter and leaving the fibres parallel. There are a number of methods of obtaining carded wool:
1. Open up the fleece by means of flicking with a metal comb through each staple
2. Use handcarders which are useful for blending fibres as well as cleaning and aerating
3. A drum carder will do large quantities called batts
4. Buying carded wool from reputable suppliers

Felting tool Rectangular piece of wood with handle

Fleece
1. The coat of wool that covers a sheep or similar animal
2. The shorn coat of the sheep, as removed after shearing

Full Using hot and cold water to thicken and shrink fibres into a firm material

Grosgrain A ribbed ribbon

Gunya Small Aboriginal shelter

Matchstick blind Fine cane blind

Nuno-felting Felting onto cloth background

Pad Layers of fleece laid at right angles to each other

Resist Material used to separate fibres so that they will not be felted together. Soft synthetic curtain fabric is best.

Ridging The creases which appear across the pad when rolled up

Rolag Fibre combed and rolled in hand carders

Roving 1. Slivers of fibre formed into slightly twisted strands ready for spinning; 2. Similar to tops, commercially prepared fleece in long strips

Slivers Continuous band of loose, untwisted fibre ready for rovings.

Staple A small piece taken from the fleece; many staples make up the whole fleece

Tops Long rolags commercially prepared

Bibliography/further reading

Austin, Bridget, *The Felter's Handbook*, Pitman, London 1988

Belgrave, Anne, *How To Make Felt*, Search Press, London

Brown, Victoria, *Feltwork*, Lorenz Books, London 1996

Burkett, Mary E., *The Art of the Feltmaker*, Abbott Hall Art Gallery, Kendal, Cumbria, UK, 1979

Chamberlain, Marcia & Crockett, Candace, *Beyond Weaving* (see chapter on felting)

Dibbs, Kristine, *Machine Embroidery Book*, Simon & Schuster, Sydney 1991

Donald, Kay, *Feltmaking*, Kangaroo Press, Sydney 1983

Eve, I., *Feltmaking, Techniques and Projects*, Lark Books 1987

Felt/filt, Lene Nielsens bi-annual magazine, $18.50 including postage, Mosejev 13, K9600 Aars, Denmark, phone/fax 00114598656322

Freeman, Sue, *Felt Craft*, Greenhouse Publications, Melbourne 1988

Ghol, E.P.G. & Vilensky, L.D., *Textiles for Modern Living* (5th ed), Longman Cheshire, London 1993

Goodman, Chris, *Making Felt is Fun*, 1984

Gordon, Beverly, *Feltmaking*, Watson-Guptill Publications, New York 1980

Mayer, Anita Luvera, *Handwoven Clothing, Felted to Wear*, Shuttle Craft Books, Couperville WA (USA) 1988

Pufpaff, Suzanne, compiler, *The Nineteenth Century Hat Makers and Felters Manuals*, includes reprints of *The Hat Makers Manual* (1829), *A Treatise on Hat-Making and Felting* by John Thomson (1868), and prints from *L'Art de Faire des Chapeaux* by Jean Antoine Nollet (1765), plus new explanations, notes, index and resources. This book can be purchased directly from Suzanne Pufpaff, 5038 E. Quimby Road, Nashville MI 49073, USA, email-feltlady@mvcc.com or from various specialty book dealers

Smith, Sheila & Walker, Frida, *Feltmaking, the Whys and Wherefores*, Dalefelt Publications, 2 Helsington Road, Kendal, Cumbria LA9 5JR UK

Spark, Patricia, *Fundamentals of Felt Making—Scandinavian-style Felting*, Shuttle Craft Books, Couperville WA (USA) 1992

BOOK SUPPLIERS

Magnolia Books
16 King Street
Balmain NSW 2041
(02) 9810 6639
Mail order books and magazines on felting

Mill Hill Books (Russ Siddall)
PO Box 4
Montville Qld 4560
(074) 429 833

The Book Connection
PO Box 583
Dubbo NSW 2830
(068) 82 3311
fax (068) 82 9535

TUTORS

Australia
Clare Caroline
1/13 McClelland Street
Willoughby NSW 2068
(02) 9958 6799
Waverly–Woollahra Arts Centre

Liz Calnan
28c Chester Street
Epping NSW 2121
(02) 9868 2753
Beginner & advanced felting

Jan Clements
PO Box 108
Yackandandah Vic 3749
(060) 27 1320
(060) 27 1533 (AH)
Hats, 3D dollmaking

Jan Clifford
20 Elizabeth Street
Murray Bridge SA 5253
Community arts

Lyn Coffill
17 Cavell Avenue
Rhodes NSW 2138
NSW 2138
(02) 9736 1501

Joyce Darley
'Golden Valley'
Old Coramba Rd
Dorrigo NSW 2453
Felt tutor

Carol Divall
PO Box 874
Goulburn NSW 2580
Fibre design

Jenni Farrell
RMB 109 Cotter Road
Weston Creek ACT 2611
(06) 288 4947
Boots/3D/ all felting

Joan Fisher
13 Eastbank Avenue
Cabramatta NSW 2166
(02) 9728 1795
Felt tutor

Val Gilmour
24 Tuart Street
Bunbury WA 6230
Felt tutor

Cheryl Gregory
RMB 113 Cotter Road
Weston Creek ACT 2611
(06) 288 9511
Preschool to Year 10—Felting in schools

Jenny Hopper
5 Figtree Drive
Diamond Beach NSW 2430
(065) 59 2889
Beginner felters & more advanced

Jenny House
'Wong Wong'
Watheroo WA 6513

Sonia Lewis
Boab–Feltworks
PO Box 321
Burwood WA 6100
(09) 362 5126

Mollie Littlejohn
19 Chittunga Road
Eden Hills SA 5050
(08) 827 5469
Rugs, garments, hats

Glennys Mann
9 Hannaford Avenue
Tamworth, NSW 2340
(067) 66 3596
Textile artist, teacher

Rachael Meek
'Old Woman's Creek'
Garland via Lyndhurst NSW 2797
(063) 451 251
Adult workshops

Mary Naylor
8 Colosseum Crescent
Baulkham Hills NSW 2153
(02) 9674 4013
Fibre artist, felter

Holly Nutley
6 Mulgara Street
Australind WA 6230

Barbara Raymond
PO Box 326
Gulgong NSW 2852
(063) 74 1881
Hats, etc

Phillipa Rooke
355 Simpsons Road
Bardon Qld 4065
(07) 3369 2003
Just about anything

Susan Seaman
RDM 169
Busselton WA 6280
Tutor

Judith Shaw
30 Pascoe Street
Karrinyup WA 6018
Felt tutor

Christine Sloan
The Old Schoolhouse Wool Workshop
Belinda Street
Gerringong NSW 2534
(042) 340 422
Beginning & advanced felting

Helen Stumkat
Cashmere Cottage
208 James Street
Toowoomba Qld 4350
(07) 39 2201
Heirloom creations

Kris Supierz
22 Eastbank Avenue
Lansvale NSW 2166
(02) 9727 0068
Private and group lessons

Pat Surace
PO Box 394
Forster NSW 2428
(065) 542 147
Fibre artist; all classes of felting

Martien Van Zuilen
20 Davies Street
Preston Vic 3072
phone/fax (03) 9484 6114
Felt tutoring at all levels, all subjects

Bubbles Warren
Jerdacuttup
via Ravensthorpe WA 6364

Eileen Wright
'Carinya'
Kings Creek Road
Krambach NSW 2429
(065) 591 258
Beginning & advanced felting

New Zealand
Bridget Austin
100 Korokoro Road
Korokoro
Lower Hutt
04-589-1678
*National tutor. All levels of felting from
    beginners to advanced.
Felting boards available at NZ$12 plus
    p&p*

Marie Harding
9 Crown Hill
Onepoto
Titahi Bay 6006
Wellington

Pat Old
Speedy Road
RD 1
Hamilton

Dreyn Pittar
69 Boucher Avenue
Te Puke 3071

Jeanne Taylor
c/- Riuaka Store
Motueka 716

United Kingdom
Jeanette Appleton
4 Almshoe Bury Cottages
near St Ippolyts
Hitchin
Herts SG4 7NS
01462 45 7669

Liz Rice
Mordyston Farm Bungalow
Dalcross
Inverness IV1 2JQ
Scotland
01463-794571
Feltmaker and teacher

United States
Beth Beede
64 Rivell Road
Northampton MA 01060
(413) 584-2950
*Lectures and workshops on felt and
    feltmaking*

Dale Liles
2142 Cherokee Blvd
Knoxville TN 37919
1-614-525-5941

Suzanne Pufpaff
'The Felt Lady'
5038 E. Quimby Road
Dept N
Nashville MI 49073-9716
517-852-1870
email feltlady@mvcc.com
*Available throughout the year for work-
    shops and demonstrations. She has
    also written a number of articles avail-
    able in reprint form. Contact for cur-
    rent listing of available articles and
    workshops.*

Patricia Spark
1032 SW Washington Street
Albany OR 97321
1-541-926-1095
fax 1-541-926-1434
email sparl@peak.org
*Felting workshops and classes through-
    out North America*

Anne Vickrey
1-800-450-2723

Canada
Maggie Tchir
Fibre Studio
606 Victoria Street
Nelson
British Columbia V1L 4K9
(250) 352-2821 fax (250) 352-1625

Denmark
Lene Nielsen
Mosejev 13
D.K. 9600 Aars
Denmark
tel/fax +45-9865-6322

FELTING ORGANISATIONS

Australia
Canberra Feltmakers
PO Box 24
Rivett ACT 2611
(06) 288 4947

Felt West
Pascoe Street
Karrinyup WA 6018
(09) 447 5659

Handweavers & Spinners NSW
PO Box 653
Burwood NSW 2134

Handspinners & Weavers Guild
196 Mile End Road
(PO Box 163)
Torrensville SA 5031

The Queensland Spinners, Weavers &
    Dyers Group
PO Box 1271
Milton Business Centre
Milton Qld 4064

TAFTA (Janet De Boer)
PO Box 38
The Gap Qld 4061
(07) 3300 6491

The Victorian Felters
20 Davies Street
Preston Vic 3072
(03) 9484 6114

United Kingdom
The International Feltmakers' Assoc.
Sec. Joan Jones
168 Armadale Road
Ladybridge
Bolton BL4 TP
United Kingdom
01204-655 438

Newsletter of the International
    Feltmakers Assn.
Eva Kuniczak
23 Glebe Road
Kincardine-on-Forth
Alloa
Clackmannanshire PK10 4QB
Scotland
tel/fax 0259-730779

North American Felters' Network
1032 S.W. Washington Street
Albany OR 97321
USA

SUPPLIERS AND CARDING SERVICES

Australia
Alderley House Alpacas Cafe & Gallery
Leger & Libbie Tindall
Alderley House, Bucketts Way
Stroud NSW 2425
phone/fax (049) 94 5086

The Alpaca Shop
1 Bate Street
Central Tilba NSW 2546
(044) 73 7177

Australian Mohair & Wool Centre
Unit 2, 15 Aspinall Place
Musgrave
Windsor NSW 2756
(PO Box 275, Riverstone NSW 2765)
(045) 77 2570

Australian Textile Recyclers
John Laverty
Lot 6 Charles Street
Euroa Vic 3666
(057) 953 578
Dyed superfine Merino tops

Banyandah Alpacas
Dawn Perryman
PO Box 16 Oatley NSW 2223
(02) 9580 3919
and:
46 London Creek Road
Peachester Queensland
015 115 81

Bennett and Gregor
24 Seventh Street
Gawler SA 5118
(085) 222 169
Carded fleece

Black & Coloured Sheep Breeders
   Assoc Aust (NSW)
C. Foreman
'The Doran'
15 30 Laheys Creek Road
Gulgong NSW 2852
(063) 741 430
Coloured fleece—Bond, Corriedale, cross-bred; wool tops, sliver
and:

Bev Layton
'Layton Vale'
733 Bocoble Road
Mudgee NSW 2850
(063) 737 658
Carded wool

S.A. Brown Pty Ltd
2/52 Shepherd Street
Chippendale NSW 2008
(02) 9319 7343
fax (02) 9698 3186
All millinery supplies; ribbons, hat blocks, stiffeners

Gillian Campbell
295 Calf Farm Road
Mt Hunter NSW 2570
(046) 54 5332
Angora goats, kid, wool fleeces; coloured and white

Carded Mohair
S. Hart
3 Drip Lane
Cooyal Mudgee NSW 2850
(063) 735 440
Natural colours & white carded mohair

Jan Clements
PO Box 108
Yackandandah Vic 3749
(060) 27 1320
Supplier of felting rollers
Carding Capers
Pamela J. Douglas
RMB 451 Porcupine Lane
Kootingal NSW 2352
(067) 67 3379
Washing & carding & white silk tops

Cora-Lynn
Cyril Lieschke
'Cora-Lynn'
Henty NSW 2658
(069) 29 3391
Black and coloured wool; white and coloured mohair; alpaca

Doongella Custom Carding
Joan & Dave Gibbons
RMB 39 Terragon
via Murwillumbah NSW 2484
(066) 797 128
Washing & carding; carded wool; exotics

Earth Palette
Alaine & Ken Flavel
PO Box 40
Gladstone SA 5473
(086) 62 2110
Cold dyes for dyeing wool and silk

Edith & Thelma P/L
Edith Davis
77 Pitt Town Road (PO Box 73)
Kenthurst NSW 2156
(02) 9871 2027
(02) 9654 9106
Carded wool sales; spinning, weaving craft supplies

Elders Wool Stores
Spearwood WA 6163
Raw fleece

Brenda Ewell
15 Buntine Road
Wembley Downs WA 6019
Supplier for handfelters

Fabulous Fibres & Craft
Noeleen & Kate
821 Maitland Vale Road
Rosebrook NSW 2320
(049) 301 920
Selection of fibres

Fibre Design Gallery
Jane Wilson & Carol Divall
9 Montague Street
Goulburn NSW 2580
(048) 221 333
Selected supplies for fibre work

Fibre Supplies
Margot Schelling
PO Box
Gundaroo NSW 2620
(062) 36 8247
Mohair & cashmere

Fibreworks
Gill Venn
RMB 7212
Horsham Vic 3401
(053) 837 530
Wool, mohair, silk, slivers, fleece

Fields of Joy
Joy Donoghue
150 Tourist Road
Kangaroo Valley NSW 2577
(044) 64 2424
Alpaca Stud

First Edition Fibres & Yarns
PO Box 201
Euroa Vic 3666
Tel/Fax ISO 61 (0) 57 95 3578
Full range tops; sheep, cashmere, angora, mohair, silk, camel, alpaca

Gaywool Dyes
Nooramunga Road
Devenish Vic 3726
(057) 641 363
*Dyes, natural and dyed wool sliver and
    fleece*

Glenwood Fibres
295 Calf Farm Road
Mt Hunter NSW 2570
(046) 54 5332

Gorge Alpacas
Richard & Julie Bird
22 Calabash Road
Arcadia NSW 2159
(02) 9655 1122

Greatex Fibre Reactive Dyes
Judy Bourke
10 Mt Gilead Road
Thirroul NSW 2515
Non-toxic dyes for wool and silk

Bill Grenfell
15 Aspen Avenue
Terrigal NSW 2260
(043) 84 2266
Felting tools; boards

Hidden Lake Farm
Nigel and Catherine Spurling
RMB 1032 Gundaroo Road
via Bungendore NSW 2621
(06) 236 9353
*Natural coloured mohair fleece and carded
    mohair*

Hope Springs
PO Box 209
Mt Pleasant SA 5235
(085) 682 597
English Leicester wool tops

Kacoonda Enterprises
Mary & John Hart-Davies
PO Box 6
Somers Vic 3927
(059) 89 5506
Dyes and fibres; drum carders

Kraft Kolour
Factory 11
72/74 Chifley Drive
Preston Vic 3072
(03) 9484 4303
*Perigan Mothproofer; Lanasol, Lanset—
    Fabric ink & paint*

Lahey Downs
Phil & Roma Lahey
2549 Waukivory
via Gloucester NSW 2422
(065) 58 2042
Alpaca fleece

Marie's Yarns
Marie Clews
5 Kristen Place
West Pennant Hills NSW 2125
(02) 9872 1599
Beautiful yarns

Marta's Yarns
Marta Cantos
71 Patrick Street
North Clayton Vic 3168
(030 9540 0529
Dyed mohair tops

Hugh McCowatt
60 Strongs Road
Berry NSW 2535
(044) 48 6053
Felting machine

Meskills Woolstore
96 Piper Street
Kyneton Vic 3401
(053) 83 7530
Dyed Corriedale fleece and sliver

Mingga Farm
Beveridge Vic 3753
(03) 9745 2518
*Woollen feltmakers; batt; natural colours;
    dyed*

Muzzlewood
Lorraine Crawley
6 Beaumont Close
Chapman ACT 2611
(062) 88 5781
*Carded and exotic fibre; wool slivers, silk
    caps, slivers*

The Old Schoolhouse Wool Workshop
Christine Sloan
Belinda Street
Gerringong NSW 2534
(042) 340 422
(042) 341 703 (AH)
*Wool workshops; all felting needs; hat
    blocks*

Peel Ridge
Margaret Peel
Cobbitty NSW 2570
(046) 51 2216
Fibre supplies; mohair

Petlin's Spinning & Weaving Supplies
17 Cavell Avenue
PO Box R–1
Rhodes NSW 2138
(02) 9736 1501
Carders, fleece, tops

C.J. Preston
333 Flinders Lane
Melbourne Vic 3000
(03) 9621 1455
fax (03) 9621 2643
Milliner's supplies

Quick-Spin Wool
Lorraine Kent
RMB 1215 Shelford Road
Meredith Vic 3333
(03) 5286 8224
*Tops and slivers of Merino; blended felted
    batts; books, videos, tools, dyes*

Ramsfield Yarns (Snowdark)
Goulburn
35 Ross Street, Bradfordville
Goulburn NSW 2580
(048) 216 344
fax (048) 217 871
*Wool sliver & weaving yarns; white and
    coloured sliver suitable for felting*

The Real Ewe
Barbara Mundell
'Chesapeake'
Roberts Road
Werombi NSW 2570
(046) 53 1457
*Washing & carding & fleece spinning
    products; Gaywool dyes*

Bev Rennie
Lot 1221 Duckenfield Rd
Duckenfield NSW 2321
(049) 30 5515 (AH)
(049) 67 6655 (WK)
Clean coloured & white fleeces

Ridgy Didge Angoras
Janet Preston
PO Box 259
Kilmore Vic 3764
(057) 81 0349
Carded pure mohair

Sal's Wool Den
Helen O'Neil
Lot 568 Valencia Way
Maddington WA 6109

(09) 459 8442

Sanshi
89A Palmerston Street
Mosman Park WA 6012
Silk sliver and yarns

Sericus Pty Ltd
PO Box 2313
Kent Town Centre SA 5071
Coloured and natural silk yarns

The Spinners & Weavers Shop (members only!)
Jill Blackburn
'Kurrajong'
Ainslie ACT 2602
(06) 247 104
Fleece, natural, carded, exotic

Helen Stumkat
Cashmere Cottage
208 James Street
Toowoomba Qld 4350
(076) 39 2201
Fibres and yarns; craft supplies

L & L Tompkins
Laurel or Lindsay
370 South Arm Road
South Arm NSW 2460
(066) 452 083 (evenings)
Carding services; coarse crossbred to superfine Merino in sliver form; high quality carded wool

The Travellers Rest
Gay Epstein
Snowy Mountains Highway
Cooma NSW 2630
(064) 52 4422
Carded & dyed fleece

Treetops Color Harmonies
Nancy Ballesteros
6 Banwee Road
Floreat WA 6014\
(09) 387 3007
Wool, silk & mohair tops

Virginia Farm Wool Works
Jenny & Phillip Dunn
122 Annangrove Road
Annangrove NSW 2156
(02) 9654 1069
Merino tops—dyed & natural; Merino blends; superfine Merino, Polwarth,

Bond fleeces; silks, etc

Gwen Watson
4 Cubbine Road
Cunderdin WA 6407

The Wool Room
Kate Sevier
'Pleasant View'
Grenfell Road
Young NSW 2594
(063) 83 3254
Gromark, Gromark/Corriedale cross fleece

New Zealand
Ashford Handicrafts Ltd
415 West Street (PO Box 424)
Ashburton

Belex Carding
Tiverton Street
Palmerston

Feltworks
15 Woodfern Crescent
Titirangi
Auckland 7

JJ's Iron Pot Carding
Waghorne Street
PO Box 2100
Ahuriri
Napier

Rotocard
Rd 2
Nelson

Tai Tapu Wool Carders
53 Main Akaroa Highway
Tai Tapu
Canterbury
Waitangi Downs WoolCarding
State Highway 1
Ohaeawai
RD2
Kaikohe

United Kingdom
Adelaide Walker
2 Mill Yard Workshops
Oxley Mills
Ilkley Road
Otely
Yorkshire LS21 3JP

01943-850812

Wingham Wool Work
70 Main Street
Wentworth
Rotherham
South Yorkshire S62 7BR
01226-742926
Suppliers of worsted tops

United States
Ironstone Warehouse
PO Box 365
Uxbridge MA 01569
1-508-278-5838
Dyed fleece

Norsk Fjord Fibre
Noel A. Thurner
Box 271
Lexington GA 30648
1-706-743-5120
Norwegian wool

Outback Fibres
Jill Gully
PO Box 153
Hewitt TX 76643
Merino roving for felting

R.H. Lindsay Co. Wool Merchants
PO Box 218
Boston MA 02124
1-617-288-1050
Dyed and carded Romney fibre

Rovings
Box 192
Oakbank MB Canada R0E 1J0
1-800-266-5536
Felting batts, Australian Polwarth

Susan's Fiber Shop
N. 250 Hwy A
Columbus WI 53925
1-414-623-4237
Everything for felting

Woodland Woolworks
262 S. Maple Street (PO Box 400)
Yamhill OR 97148-8420
1-800-547-3725
Fibres and felting equipment

INDEX